A PLACE
WHERE DREAMS
COME TRUE

A PLACE WHERE DREAMS COME TRUE

CHUCK THOMAS

TATE PUBLISHING
AND ENTERPRISES, LLC

Published by Tate Publishing & Enterprises, LLC
127 E. Trade Center Terrace | Mustang, Oklahoma 73064 USA
1.888.361.9473 | www.tatepublishing.com

Tate Publishing is committed to excellence in the publishing industry. The company reflects the philosophy established by the founders, based on Psalm 68:11,
"The Lord gave the word and great was the company of those who published it."

Book design copyright © 2014 by Tate Publishing, LLC. All rights reserved.
Cover design by Allen Jomoc
Interior design by Jimmy Sevilleno

Published in the United States of America

ISBN: 978-1-62854-864-8
1. Religion / Christian Life / Personal Growth
2. Religion / Christian Life / Inspirational
14.08.13

ACKNOWLEDGMENTS

I WANT TO give thanks to Jesus Christ for giving me strength to share this story with you, along with my family for their loving support and encouragement. Special thanks to my wife, Pam, for loving me through the good times and the bad, and for giving me a female perspective that completed the story. I also want to thank my daughter Becky for her marathon editing and retyping sessions of this manuscript. I want to thank Ayenna, Sarah and Elizabeth for editing and Steve, Richard, Josiah, Rachel and Shirley for their evaluations. Special thanks to Sara Everett for final proofing this work.

CONTENTS

INTRODUCTION

I T IS NOT in my nature to involve myself in such a venture as writing a book. I have been encouraged by friends and family to write down how God has touched my life. I believe we all have a unique story. God desires to show us his great love by revealing himself through the stories of our lives, so when something unusual does happen, we are not surprised by the uniqueness of the God story that is being sculpted in these events. Through my family's encouragement, I have been persuaded to journal these stories, even though these intimate times in my life have seemed insignificant or caused heartache. I am grateful for the support of all my friends and family; they have been a vital part of my spiritual growth and maturity along the way. Most of all, I want to give thanks to Jesus who gives us the ability, through his grace, to do things beyond our own strength and talents. I could not have done this without him.

During my college class on the book of Acts, my professor explained that Acts is a history of the actions of the Apostles and the church. She said the book is still being written today in the lives of those who are now living, and it will continue to be written until Jesus receives his bride for the marriage supper of the Lamb (Rev. 19:9). This is my prayer—that God would reveal his acts in my life for his glory and for the encouragement of those who will read the words of this book.

SLAP OF REALITY

I T WAS GRADUATION day for the class of 1977. I was an eighteen-year-old walking out of my graduation ceremony toward the school cafeteria with the final strains of "Pomp and Circumstance" lingering in the background. Thoughts raced through my head, *What am I going to do now?* Up until this point in my life, everything had been dictated to me. As a kid, having no adult responsibilities, there was no need of thought given to the daily cares of life. Now all of a sudden, the weight of this responsibility was on my shoulders. A wave of panic swept over me. I thought, *Man, I have to start getting serious about life.* At that moment, I hit the wall of reality.

Growing up in Iowa, I had a typical Midwestern life. I grew up in a God-fearing, non-Christian family. We attended church two or three times a year, but the mention of God never came up unless someone we knew had died. In the late-70s, I was doing the same things as most other teenagers. I was involved with high school activities, parties, and hanging out with friends at the local bowling alley. My life was a routine; it felt like a machine. Deep down, I knew something was missing. I knew there had to be more to life than sucking up air and taking up space. Something inside me said there had to be a higher purpose to our existence.

During my childhoood, I watched old movies like *Ben Hur*, *The Ten Commandments*, and *The Robe*. I saw the faith in the main characters. I knew they had something I wanted, but I didn't know how to attain it. This thought lurked in the back of my mind; I had a desire to know the answers to all these questions of faith.

When I was older, I started watching the TV series *The Waltons*. I loved the series because of the family's closeness. I admired how they loved and supported one another in bad times and in good times. I coveted that for my own family; it was my heart's desire to have a family that close. It was a dream.

I remember grabbing a Bible and heading outside on a warm autumn day when I was in my early teens. I found the old Chinese elm tree on the north side of our white two-story home on Cedar Street. The house was on top of the limestone bluffs that ran along the river in Iowa Falls, Iowa. With my Bible shoved in my pocket, I climbed to a high branch, sat down and leaned against the trunk. A strong wind blew as it commonly does in Iowa, and I started praying, "God, if you're for real, I would like to hear your voice like Ben Hur and Moses did." Sitting there feeling the wind and watching it stir up waves on the Iowa River below, I felt a peace in my heart that everything was going to be all right. When I opened the Bible, I flipped to the book of Joel chapter 2 verses 28–32, where God says:

> I will pour out my Spirit on all people. Your sons and daughters will prophesy, your old men will dream dreams, and your young men will see visions. Even on my servants, both men and women, I will pour out my Spirit in those days. I will show wonders in the heavens and on the earth, blood and fire and billows of smoke. The sun will be turned

to darkness and the moon to blood before the coming of the great and dreadful day of the Lord. And everyone who calls on the name of the Lord will be saved; for on Mount Zion and in Jerusalem there will be deliverance, as the Lord has said, among the survivors whom the Lord calls.

These verses spoke life into my spirit; the passage seemed as if it were jumping off the pages—as if what I was reading had life. I felt the words speaking directly to me; this was the first time I experienced anything like that. I didn't hear God's audible voice but knew deep down that he had everything under control. I felt so peaceful.

Most people want to leave an influential mark on this earth in some way—to make their lives count for something greater than themselves. From that moment on, I wanted my life to have influence and to make a difference. Deep down in my heart, there was a desire to leave an eternal mark in the lives of others. If Moses could influence a nation of people with God's help, then I could do the same by getting to know the same God. *So where do I begin?*

THE BEGINNING

I WAS BORN with an identical twin in Bishop, California, in October of 1958. We were named after our two grandfathers, Charles Thomas and Edward Keesey. My mom managed us, along with my older brother, Lanny, who had been born a year and a half earlier. Our mother, Shirley, loved us, and we never had reason to doubt that. Needless to say, at that time it was quite a task to raise three young boys in a small miners' community stuck between the high Sierras and the White Mountains in Inyo County. Our dad worked in the mineral mines in the area. My parents were born and raised in Iowa and had been invited by my dad's uncle to come work and live in California. My father, Charles Ray, found his new job boring. Mom said he had a hard time staying awake watching buckets of minerals come up on a conveyor, and because of that, he later lost his job. So after a year and a half in California, we headed to Colorado. Dad worked in the mines again, so we only lived there for a short stint. We then moved back to Iowa where my youngest brother, Blaine, was born.

Now with a family of six, Dad got a new job in the local grocery store chain in Creston, Iowa. My grandparents lived there, so they helped Mom take care of us. Eventually, my dad was transferred to Iowa Falls, Iowa, and that's where we spent the next twenty years.

When I was growing up, I felt insecure and unsure of myself. I know it was due to how each one of my brothers and I related to our dad. My childhood memories of my dad were difficult. He was considerably self-involved, and our family life was determined by what he wanted to do. My mother didn't have a choice in family matters. She may have had input and probably did, but it came across to me that Dad had all the control. He loved us and provided for us, but I felt like whatever I did wasn't good enough.

I held resentment toward my father because I wanted peace in our family, and there rarely was. My brothers and I didn't want to do anything to make him mad, so our home life was full of tension. During the school year, I dreaded the weekend because I would have to spend it trying to manage his angry outbursts. When things didn't go his way, he would make everyone's life a living hell; it made me so mad. This bullying was his form of manipulation to get people to do what he wanted them to do. He was selfish. I couldn't wait to grow up and be out on my own. I dreamed about being old enough to leave the house and start my own life. Sometimes while he was in one of his rants downstairs, I fervently wished I could just get out of there and go live with my friends. I wanted to escape.

No child should have to feel that way. Every kid craves acceptance. It is in a child's nature to please his parents. My dad would seldom acknowledge the good work or the effort put into the jobs we did. He just expected work to be done; and if it weren't, there would be hell to pay. Even if we did everything correctly, there was no positive appreciation. Panic would devour me if we were asked to do a job. If we broke a tool or something didn't go as planned, there would be an explosion of anger because we had just ruined everything. It was such bondage, and I hated it with all my heart.

I felt like I was living in a concentration camp, and it seemed to be worse in our teen years when all these personal issues with my dad came to a climax. He was unhappy, and he struggled with depression. Many nights as we sat down for supper, my dad would talk only to my mom. If we had anything to say, we had to talk to Mom. With Mom acting as the mediator, she would then repeat what we had said to him and vice versa. When he came home from work, Mom told us he was home, and we went down to the basement to avoid conflict. Later on, we found out that this made him more upset. Life should be better than this, and I was determined to find the answer. My searching started here.

I wanted to do things right. Being a perfectionist, I always worked to get flawless papers in school and would be overly frustrated with myself when I didn't attain the A. Constantly this conflict chafed my mind. I thought of myself as "screwed up" because I wanted to do better. This insecurity fostered fear. I never chose to take risks for fear of failure. I didn't like myself, and I couldn't understand how anyone could like me because of my imperfections. If there were a God, there had to be a better way of living life; but again, I had no idea where to begin. In my teen years of watching the Waltons deal with life's issues, I envied them very much. They lived a dream life, and I wanted my family to be exactly like theirs.

As I became older, I grew more and more emotionally needy; I sought relationships with girls to fill that void. When my girl-friends told me they liked me, I could never figure out why. I did not even like myself, so how could anyone else like me? In an effort to feel fulfilled, I spent most of my time with my girl-friends. As a single guy, I longed to be emotionally connected to a girl. Getting completely infatuated and wrapped up in these relationships was what I did because I had no idea who I was. The lack of affirmation from my dad led me to look outside the family for love and acceptance. Working on cars and engines was another thing I loved to do. My passion to fix things paralleled my passion to fix my life. I was never alone but always looking. I became emotionally dependent.

THE SEARCHING

SOMEWHERE IN THE midst of those twenty years, I had a growing desire to find the purpose of my existence. Even as a nonbeliever, my logical mind knew there had to be more than just eating, sleeping, and working. I couldn't get past the fact that everything around me screamed, "There's got to be a bigger plan." I didn't make a connection at the time, but later after reading the Bible, I saw in Romans chapter 1:20, "For since the creation of the world God's invisible qualities—his eternal power and divine nature—have been clearly seen, being understood from what has been made, so that men are without excuse." Even at a young age, I did not understand how anyone could not believe in God. I knew it didn't matter what I went through because every time I looked up at the stars, I saw there had to be someone who made this amazing universe.

The few times we attended church, I experienced some measure of peace. Even though I didn't understand it, I knew there was something right about it all. God was planting seeds in me to guide my way before I realized what *the way* was. I felt as if he was honoring my hunger to know the truth and to see the bigger picture.

GENUINE CHRISTIANS

DURING THE PAIN and struggle of growing up, compounded with the normal insecurities, there came a time in junior high when our church hired a new associate pastor, Kermit Culver. We were told he came to our church to help with the youth, which brought a sense of excitement to me. The church had never hired someone who worked directly with the youth, and he seemed like a guy who genuinely cared for people. He was different, more at peace than an average person. That serenity alone was enough to draw me to him; there was something about him I wanted in my own life. After a week or so, we received a phone call. It was Kermit. He wanted to come over and hang out with our family. I thought that was really cool because I wanted to get to know this guy.

An hour later I heard a knock at the door, and there was our associate pastor in his shorts and t-shirt holding a basketball. "Would you guys like to play some basketball?" My brothers and I scrambled out the door and jogged up the street to the local courts. Kermit's intentions were clear. He just came over to hang out. He wasn't trying to cram religion down our throats; he just wanted to be one of the guys. Every time we talked, he was genuine and soft-spoken. He shared everyday things about his faith and what Jesus meant to him. Kermit never talked about Jesus in the past tense. Kermit was the first person I knew who saw Jesus as a friend. His faith was so practical and real. I never thought anyone could have a daily, intimate relationship with Jesus. That day at the basketball courts was the very first time I genuinely wanted to know Jesus.

Kermit was passionate about preaching. He would talk about how much he enjoyed being able to present God's Word and its truth. I remember one time when we drove back from a weekend retreat, Kermit was talking about his preaching. In the middle of our conversation, Kermit turned and looked at me and said, "Chuck, have you ever thought about being a preacher?"

I said, "No way would I ever want to preach and do what you do."

Kermit just looked at me and smiled; it was almost as if he knew something I didn't. I had a paralyzing fear of public speaking; however, God used Kermit's words to plant a seed of faith in me. It was as if God was looking at me and saying, "Wait and see."

As I said, in high school I started looking to relationships to fill the emptiness I felt inside. I turned to friends and girls to fill that void. I needed to have something to hang onto outside of myself because I didn't like being alone. Solitude was a hollow, empty feeling. I would tell myself, "There has to be more. Life has to have a greater purpose." I didn't know any better, and I kept doing the only thing I knew how to do: I followed the crowd and tried to fit in.

My senior year, I was dating a girl who was a Christian. We had met through play practice, and she invited me to go with her to a youth meeting. I thought it was probably just a bunch of fake Christian people who were against drinking, swearing, and dating—people who sat around and sang "Kumbaya." I went with her so she would stop hassling me about it. I thought I'd go once; then she would be quiet. It was a Sunday night, and I suggested we arrive late so we could skip all of the singing and praying. When we walked in the door late, they were still singing; and they hadn't started praying yet. I was thinking this was going to be a long, boring night. But the meeting wasn't too bad. The people were friendly and curious about a new visitor. It was nice to feel that people really cared about me and who I was. This was the first time I had experienced such a genuine welcome.

CONVERSION

ONE EVENING, I took my girlfriend home after a day out, and as we were sitting in my car outside of her house, we were talking about the world and how bad things seemed to be. She said, "As bad as things are, I will sure be happy when Jesus comes back and takes us home."

I said to her, "When Jesus comes back, what do you mean... when Jesus comes back?"

She said, "Yeah, Jesus is going to come back again." I had never heard this before. In all my life, I had never heard that Jesus is coming back a second time to take the Christians home. This was a new twist, and I decided to take some time to find out the rest of the story.

My girlfriend asked me, "Chuck... are you a Christian?"

"Well... I think so," I hedged.

Then she said, "What makes you think so?"

"Well, I believe in God, and I haven't murdered anyone, and I go to church occasionally," I said. She then explained that those things weren't enough and that Jesus says that you must be born again to enter the kingdom of heaven. She explained I must repent, turn from my sins, and invite Jesus to be Lord of my life. I asked, "How do I do this?"

She responded, "With a simple prayer. Just say, 'Jesus, forgive me for my sins, cleanse me, make me right with you. I ask you to take up residence in me and make me a new person.'"

I thought, *Wow it's just that simple, no work, no religious duty. There has to be more to this.*

She said, "It's just a starting point. God sends his Holy Spirit to teach you his ways and to lead you into all truth" (John 16:13).

Could this be true? Could this be what I was looking for... the answers to my emptiness? I had a feeling this was the answer to all my questions, and I couldn't wait to get home. By this time in our conversation, I was getting really excited. I told her I needed to go home, so we parted ways.

When I arrived home, I felt great anticipation and excitement about the new truth revealed to me. I pulled the car up in the driveway and hurried up to the house feeling as if I had just found the greatest treasure, but not yet knowing what was in the treasure box. Knowing I could have an intimate relationship with the living God and his Holy Spirit was fantastic. I had no hesitations; I knew God knew more than I knew myself, and he saw the whole picture.

I stepped into my house with expectancy in my heart, and I made my way downstairs into the basement family room. I got down on my knees and prayed, "Jesus, if you're for real, I ask you to forgive me for all my sins. I am sorry for what I have done. I know you are God and you hear me. I am inviting you in."

At that moment, I felt the power of his touch on my body; it felt as if I were electrically charged. I had goose bumps all over and the sensation that everything was being made clean. In thankfulness, my hands shot up. With my arms lifted, I began to praise the Lord and thank him for his wonderful gift. I was ecstatic. I knew something had changed in me, and I had something my friends and family had not experienced. I proceeded up the stairs and walked into the kitchen where my mother was preparing dinner. I stepped up behind her and said, "Mom, I just accepted Jesus into my heart, and I think I have found what I'm looking for."

"That's wonderful. I am so glad for you," she said. I proceeded to tell her what had happened earlier in the day—how I was led to my decision to follow Jesus. She could see the expression on my face and excitement in my voice, and she knew that something had definitely changed in me.

The next day, I woke up with a greater sense of his presence, and I felt a deep joy that I knew was not originating within me. I could not contain the joy that I felt. I had to tell people what Jesus had just done in me. I started telling everyone I saw. This feeling continued for many weeks. It was a genuine affection for Jesus that had emotionally time-stamped me, and it was a dream come true.

THE NEXT STEP

AFTER A FEW months had passed, my strong fervor for the Lord had diminished some, though I knew that something had changed in me. I was still doing some of the old things I had done before I became a Christian, but I must admit, the desire to do these things was not as strong as it had been before. There were still changes that needed to happen for me to be more fulfilled.

A couple of months later, I knew I was different on the inside, but my actions had yet to follow. I was still living the same lifestyle as before, but one particular night I felt a great desire to start reading the Bible. Not having an understanding why, I went into my room and found my Bible. I walked back into the family room where my parents sat watching TV, and I plopped on the couch and cracked open the Bible for the first time. It opened to Matthew chapter five where Jesus lays out the Beatitudes. Jesus is talking about how Christians should live their lives. As I began to read, it was like a lamp was illuminating the words.

The words were alive, and for the first time in my life, they actually made sense. I felt like a dry sponge soaking up the water of truth after living in the desert all my life. It was amazing; the words seemed to jump off the page, and I was overwhelmed with gratefulness. It was like finding the treasure I had been looking for all my life. Jesus was talking about being the salt and light of the world, fulfilling the law, loving your enemy, and forgiving all those who hurt you. These words spoke to my heart and my mind about what I must become. That night, a switch flipped on in me, and my thinking started to change.

THE FIRST BATTLE

I'VE LEARNED THROUGHOUT life that for every good action, there is an equal and opposite reaction. Jesus opened up his word to me, and a dynamic change began. Yet at the same time, the enemy had his own plan to knock down and block the plan of God. On the same night I was reading the Bible for the first time, the phone rang. My mom answered it but quickly passed it to my dad. I could hear my dad's conversation: "He what?... Hit a train?... What do you mean?... I can't believe this!" Then he slammed down the phone in anger and said, "Ed drove into a parked train and wrecked the car. That was the police." My dad was furious. He looked at me and barked, "Come on! Let's go!" We ran up the stairs for jackets, then out to the garage for a crowbar and hammer. These we threw in the back of the truck.

As we drove out to the accident, my dad grumbled in anger. I was afraid to ask him any questions, so I kept quiet the whole drive there. I could see that this would not be a good night. When we got to the accident, my dad jumped out of the truck in a tirade. He was yelling at my brother, "What were you doing?" "What were you thinking?" and "How stupid can you be?" All of this tongue-lashing was laced with profanity and anger. The police and everyone else at the crash site stood around listening and watching. Dad was out of control. Ed stood there and took the abuse. My dad wasn't concerned about whether or not Ed had been hurt in the accident. All he was concerned about was the damage to the car and how this was making him look bad. Finally, the police calmed my dad down and got him focused. We began to work on bending the driver side fender away from the tire so the car could be driven.

While this was going on, something greater was at work in me. Normally, I would have experienced anger welling up inside, but instead I felt as if I were living above the intense storm. I was isolated and protected from the emotional pain of the event. Once we got the fender of the car straightened out, my dad said, "Chuck, you drive the car home." Without saying a word, I got into the car and drove it home. I parked the car and went into the house to wait for the evening to unfold.

It wasn't much longer before my dad was home with my brother. They came into the house, and my dad was still ranting and raving about the accident. This went on for quite some time; my dad had no restraint. He was coming unglued. I was downstairs in the basement family room listening to the war raging upstairs. The moment still felt surreal because even in the chaos, I was living above the pain of it all. Looking back, I can see how it was part of the plan of darkness. Satan wanted to destroy all that God was doing in me. Suddenly, I felt compelled to go upstairs and tell my dad how I felt about him. I didn't know what was going to come out of my mouth when I approached my dad, but I knew I had to talk with him.

When I got to the top of the steps and rounded the corner, I saw my mom and dad standing in the doorway between the kitchen and dining room. By this time, my brother had already * gone to his room. I walked up to my dad and said, "Dad, there has been a change in me. I'm a Christian now, and I just want you to know, no matter what happens, I will always love you." He just stood there in disbelief. I couldn't believe what I was saying. I knew this was a God thing.

Then he sputtered, "Love… what do you mean love? We're not talking about love." He then turned away from me to continue his ranting and raving. At that moment, I knew for sure that something was different. I was not the man I used to be. There was something bringing me comfort in the midst of this storm, and I was totally awed. My twin brother had been listening downstairs. He told me later that this was the night he knew something had changed in me, and he wanted whatever I had in his own life. He accepted Jesus that night and surrendered his heart. God took what the devil meant for our family's destruction, and he used it—not for destruction but for expansion in the kingdom of God.

Shortly after Ed's encounter with the train, my mother made Jesus Lord of her life. She told me that she had received Jesus as a child and realized that she needed God in her everyday life because of the positive changes God had created in my life. She later told my dad he was no longer number one in her life, and that she had to make room for Jesus in her heart because God was now number one. That statement shook my dad's world. For the first time in his life, he felt as if he were losing control of his family because of this Jesus thing.

Time passed, and I kept reading the Bible and growing in faith. Things were still difficult with my dad, but I saw God working.

HEAVENLY LANGUAGE

I T WAS TIME for me to think about college. I had an interest in fine arts, so I enrolled at the local community college as an art illustration major. I found a room in the home of an elderly woman who lived on campus. She rented out second floor bedrooms of her old, white house to enrolled college students. She was a God-fearing woman, and we spent some afternoons talking about Jesus and his second coming. She had quite a history and had the gift of hospitality when it came to college students. There were two bedrooms upstairs, and she would house two boys in each room like a dorm room but in a smaller setting. The times I had alone, I would spend reading the Bible, learning a great deal about myself and how much I needed Jesus in my life. Reading the Bible also created an urgency in me to tell others about what I was learning. I would find myself talking about my relationship with Jesus to others, and they would ask me questions that helped me to search the Scriptures and find answers to their questions. It was an exciting time.

One weekend during fall semester, I was reading in 1 Corinthians 12 about the gifts of the Holy Spirit. I had not started attending a church regularly, and I didn't know there were such things as the gifts of the Holy Spirit. All I knew was God had put his Holy Spirit in me, and those gifts were in me for his good use. I had already come to the realization that God was using me as a mouthpiece. When I talked to people about Jesus, it felt as if someone else were talking. Jesus was speaking through me as I testified about my life. It was obvious by people's responses that they perceived a change in me. I found it amazing that he would use someone who didn't think much of himself as a mouthpiece of his truth. In the 1 Corinthians passage, the writer was encouraging the church to desire earnestly greater gifts. I concluded that all of the gifts listed are given to any person who desires them and who is willing to be humble and ask for them. That is exactly what I did.

I was fascinated with the gift of speaking in other tongues. All the other gifts were cool, but I wanted this one first. Through my reading, I learned that God is willing, by a spirit of grace, to give us what we desire. 1 Corinthians 12:4-6 says, "There are different kinds of gifts, but the same Spirit. There are different kinds of service, but the same Lord. There are different kinds of working, but the same God works all of them in all men." I yearned for this gift, and God saw my desire.

Grabbing my Bible one evening, I went downstairs and stepped outside the house. I could feel a warm, southern breeze whisking across my face. It was a perfect night; leaves rustled in the wind, and a warm, star-filled sky canopied above me. I walked over to the east side of the house where some old, wooden cellar doors rested right next to the foundation. I gently lay down on those doors, which gave me a great view of the starlit night above. While looking up toward heaven, I began reaching for the stars with my hands lifted up. I said to the Lord, "I know you want to give me this gift, and I want to be able to speak in tongues. So,

Lord, I am going to speak by faith a few syllables that won't make any sense. This is my step in faith. As I speak, I ask you for this gift of tongues."

I began to speak two and three letter syllables like *ki, ra, de,* over and over again. While I was doing this, thoughts like *This is not going to work,* and *Your roommate will come down here and hear your babbling and ask you what you're doing* ran through my mind. I didn't care; I was determined to receive this gift. I had resolved to stay there until I received the gift. I kept repeating the same syllables over and over again for a couple of minutes. Then suddenly, I started hearing more syllables and, as time went on, even more. Now I began getting excited, and because of my excitement, the volume increased. My roommate walked out the door, and then he came over. "What are you doing out here?"

By that time, I was so excited and I blurted out, "I just got tongues!" My roommate thought it was crazy, but at this point in time, I didn't care what he thought. I had received something special from Jesus, and no one could take it away from me. As the evening wore on, I kept speaking in my new language and thanking God. When I went to bed, I was concerned that in the morning I would not be able to speak in this language again. So, I climbed into bed and spoke in tongues until I fell asleep. The next morning when I woke up, I thought, *Can I still speak in tongues?* I began to speak the syllables again, and it was as if I'd never stopped. The gift was still mine.

That same morning in my biology class, I told my best friend, Gary Beer, I had received the gift of tongues. He replied, "Let me hear it." When class was over, we went down to an empty lab room, and I softly spoke the new language to him so he could hear it. He said, "That's pretty cool." It was a strong example to Gary that God was real. Not long after this, Gary approached me and reported he had accepted Christ. It was truly amazing to me how God was working in other people as he was working in me.

That was God's intent from the very beginning, that we live our lives connected to him; and because of that connection, we will produce fruit, and soon other people will see the fruit and want Jesus too. If the fruit is attractive, others will want some. You don't have to be something you're not; you are what he makes you. That's what the Lord was showing me at this time in my life; it's about knowing him and being changed through that relationship with him that will cause good to happen all around you. It was an exciting way to live, and it was a whole lot better than the life I gave up and left behind.

THE SPIRIT OF RELIGION

I HAD BEEN attending an on-campus Bible study led by a local pastor. I was completely ignorant of the different beliefs of denominations and was still excited about speaking in tongues. It did not occur to me that this was something I needed to hide. In my ignorance, I began sharing with others at the study what God had just done in my life. As I was walking and conversing, I passed by the preacher who was listening to me. His ears seemed to perk up when I mentioned I had received tongues; for as soon as he heard me mention the word *tongues*, he sprang up from his chair, put his face in mine, and began to raise his voice and tell me how I was wrong. He said I was speaking of the devil, and I was deceived.

Looking back, I believe that as a minister, he was off-base in the way he publicly handled the situation, shocking me with this confrontation. I thought that everybody felt the way I did about God and about the gifts of the Holy Spirit. Because I wasn't raised in the church, this kind of attack was strange to me. Naïvely, I believed every minister felt the same way about the gifts of the Holy Spirit. I was more dismayed at his display of anger, pride, and the lack of fruit of the Holy Spirit. But I knew this one thing: this new gift I had received was real, and no person or church doctrine was going to change my mind. It also confirmed to me that the devil was angry and this was an attack to try to instill doubt about my newfound gift.

The remainder of the meeting was spent answering questions my friends were asking me about tongues. These conversations lasted throughout the entire semester, and that same minister would occasionally try to eavesdrop on our conversations. It didn't matter; God was still moving in the lives of people in that Bible study, and that made me excited.

THE SCHOOL OF GOD

CONTENT WITH THE direction my life was going, school became secondary to me. What God was doing in my life was so much more important. I had changed from a person who looked for fulfillment in relationships with other people to someone who was learning that a relationship with Jesus is the only thing that matters. In the past, I thought emotional attachments would fulfill me and make me a better person. But every time a relationship crashed, I would crash. I hated living like that. I felt enslaved to other people. I hated the emptiness of those "destined to crash and burn" connections. There had to be more. So after my last "crash and burn" experience I said to Jesus, "This is it… it's just you and me now, Lord, so show me the right way to go."

Knowing if I got close to the Lord and made him a priority in my life he would make things turn out for the better, from that time on, I stopped looking to other people for answers to life's questions and turned to the Word of God instead. I wanted more of God and less of myself. That became my motto. Before reading the Bible, I would pray and ask Jesus to reveal his truth to me. It was amazing; as the days went on, he showed me more truths in his word that changed my life and my thinking. It was a process. I kept devouring the Word, and the Holy Spirit revealed his principles. I kept growing and learning how to live a blessed life and be more fruitful. When I went home, I sat down with my mom and brothers and told them everything God was doing and showing me. This planted seeds in their hearts, giving them a desire for more. I probably made them a little sick, bombarding them with all the good news I gave them in a short amount of time, but my zeal would not let me sit still. This time was so exciting for me, and it began to rub off on those around me. I didn't know how to act differently, so I was eager to share these revelations with those I loved.

One time when a group of us was walking around campus, my friends invited me into their house. I began to tell them all the good things God was doing in my life. They were curious and wanted to know more. Suddenly, I found myself standing in the middle of the room, Bible open, answering questions about many Biblical topics. We talked about sin, being a Christian, the second coming of Jesus, and the gifts of the Holy Spirit. God's speaking through me was evident. I loved knowing that God was using me to reach others as I was growing myself. Not only was I his student, but at the same time, I was also being a teacher. Joy filled me while I was telling other people about what God was doing. It was better than drinking with my buddies or doing some of the old things I used to do. The past seemed distant because I never thought about it. My desire to sin was leaving; not that I by my own will-power stopped sinning, but God was showing me a better life. Without my realizing it, the stuff I used to do fell off of me. I was changing because I was so enveloped in the good news.

It was an amazing time when I lived on my own. I made all my own decisions, and God had my ears, my heart, and my mind. He had me, and I was finding myself in him. I was living a dream. Matthew 7:24-25 became meaningful to me. It says:

> Therefore everyone who hears these words of mine and puts them into practice is like a wise man who built his house on the rock. The rains came down, the streams rose, and the winds blew and beat against that house; yet it did not fall, because it had its foundation on the rock.

This Scripture made sense to me because I felt so secure in the things I was learning. Directed by God, I became my own man. How can you go wrong with that combination? You can't, and I was experiencing it.

During that semester, I kept growing and seeking God. I was completely content in my relationship with him. I had peace that he was taking care of me since I was seeking his kingdom first. What a change I had gone through in one semester of college! Jesus was becoming enough for me.

FORGIVENESS

I WAS TAKING a difficult math class. It was beyond me, so I decided to drop the class. I told the Lord if I dropped the class, I would dedicate the time to prayer and study in the Bible. During this time, Jesus began to speak to me about forgiving my dad for all of the hurt and pain he had caused my family and me.

In Matthew 6:14–15 it says:

> For if you forgive men when they sin against you, your heavenly Father will also forgive you. But if you do not forgive men their sins, your Father will not forgive your sins.

When I realized how much I hurt Jesus by not forgiving my father, I began to weep uncontrollably. What I had to do was obvious. Making a card, I wrote down that I forgave my dad for everything he had done because Jesus has forgiven me for everything I had done. After I finished writing the note, I mounted my motorcycle, rode to my parents' house and put the note in the mailbox. Telling my dad face-to-face seemed impossible. My mother later told me that my father came to tears when he read the note. Knowing that brought me assurance that God was continually chipping away the dark and ugly things that were standing in the way of a deepening relationship with Christ. Jesus did a lot of house cleaning in me during that semester.

Great changes were happening in my life, and I found it hard to believe Jesus could be so intimate and personal with every detail. I continually read the Word of God, and Jesus was steadily molding my life. His love engulfed me and was so fulfilling that it was easy to forget the old way of life and grab hold of the new. Happiness was prevalent in my life, and everyone who knew me could see the difference. The Lord was leading me through a strong emotional response in order to time-stamp his mark on me so that I would not forget. I have come to realize that the things we remember in life are the great emotional ups and downs that are recorded as time moves along. Whether it is a bad experience or an extremely joyful experience, these are the times we remember.

That is why the Lord allows joyful and painful times: so he can time-stamp us. I remind myself that God sees the bigger picture. He sees my whole life from beginning to end; and if he didn't, he wouldn't be God. As Christians, we have to learn to look at the bigger picture. If we don't, we will short-circuit God's plan for good in our lives. In our desire to get short-term satisfaction, we surrender the bigger picture for a moment of sinful pleasure. This is why we must learn not to make rash decisions based on emotion but instead take time to be in God's presence and allow him to transform our minds.

Jesus takes a lifetime to teach us things we need to learn about him. It's hard to wait for God's plan to be fulfilled, but one thing I am learning about life is that he is worth the wait when we're looking with eternal eyes. God's holiness calls us to live above our circumstances. We may be going through a storm, but through God's grace we can see the big picture, so we will not be influenced by the winds and turmoil. As believers we forget that everything we do in this life, whether we do it for God or for ourselves, will be judged and set before us—not in condemnation but in eternal reward. What we do will determine how we reign and rule with him in his kingdom. If we keep these things in mind, it will influence our daily decisions.

I don't want my works to be wood, hay, and straw, which will burn up in the fire of his judgment. It is my desire, and hopefully yours, to have gold, silver, and fine jewels left after the fire has burned out.

In 1 Corinthians 3:10-15, it says:

> By the grace God has given me, I laid a foundation as an expert builder, and someone else is building on it. But each one should be careful how he builds. For no one can lay any foundation other than the one already laid, which is Jesus Christ. If any man builds on this foundation using gold, silver, costly stones, wood, hay or straw, his work will be shown for what it is, because the Day will bring it to light. It will be revealed with fire, and the fire will test the quality of each man's work. If what he has built survives, he will receive his reward. If it is burned up, he will suffer loss; he himself will be saved but only as one escaping through the flames.

The most important thing in life is not how much money we have made or how successful we are. When it is all said and done, it will be about how many people we have influenced for the kingdom of God. I tell my family the only thing you can take to heaven is people. They are the only things that matter.

LAY WITNESS MISSION

ONE MORNING WHILE in biology lab, I received a phone message from my good friend Melvin Crabtree. He wanted me to call him as soon as I could. When class was over, I called Melvin. He told me there was a lay witness mission in Fort Dodge, Iowa, at Epworth Methodist Church, and he needed a youth leader to help out. I said I would be glad to fill the position—it would be a great experience and another opportunity for me to share my faith. A lay witness mission is where believers who've had a born-again experience are invited into mainline denominational churches to give their testimonies of how they were saved and came into the kingdom of God.

Melvin picked me up at my apartment on campus for the hour-long drive to Fort Dodge. Melvin was a fun-loving person who reminded me of Santa Claus. He had a jolly laugh that came from his belly, and his joy of the Lord was infectious. Mel loved people, and he was always thinking about reaching other people for Jesus. I was nervous about the weekend because this was my first time in formal ministry. I had a fear of public speaking, and I was hesitant to give my testimony in front of a large group of people. At the same time, I knew how the Holy Spirit worked in the lives of people, and I was anticipating Jesus' doing some wonderful things.

The car rolled up to the church, and we piled out. The building was a traditional brick-built Methodist church with the high pinnacles and a bell tower. After a few minutes, more mission workers flooded through the door laughing and having a good time. It didn't take me long to notice two blonde girls. There was something different about these girls; they weren't giggly adolescents. These two girls seemed mature and strong in their faith. It was a breath of fresh air to see some girls with a genuine joy and spiritual presence about them. They had a joy that I hadn't seen in any young ladies since I had become a Christian, and it was refreshing.

The leaders called us together for personal introductions, and we each told a brief story of how Jesus had changed our lives. We could sense the Holy Spirit speaking through each one as we told our stories. God was breaking down the walls in our audience's hearts as people responded to the ministry of the Holy Spirit. While the ministry was going on, I kept noticing these two blonde girls, Pam and Nancy Pagel, from Clare, Iowa. When I looked at them, they were looking at me. I was intrigued and found myself staring at them, curious to know more.

As the weekend came to a close, Nancy and Pam invited me over for a visit sometime in the next month so I could get to know them and their family. It was great to know some people who were committed to Jesus like me, and I was looking forward to getting to know the rest of the family and hear what God was doing in them.

THE MOTORCYCLE RIDE AND THE FARM

A FEW WEEKS after the lay witness mission, I was back at school, and everything was going well. The time for my visit to the Pagel farm was quickly approaching, but my only problem was I didn't have a car that ran. All I had was a motorcycle, which I had already winterized. Most of my travels were on my motorcycle or on foot at the time. My parents lived in the same town, and everything was within walking distance or, at least, motorcycle distance. A new obstacle was rising; it was cold. I had to travel about sixty-five miles to the girls' house, so I had to find a car to borrow for the weekend. My friend Gary had a car, so I asked him if I could use his car for the weekend if I reimbursed him for gas. He told me that would be fine, so things were set for my great adventure. I could hardly wait for the weekend.

On Saturday morning, I heard a knock at my door. It was Gary. He said his mother had changed her mind and didn't want me driving his car over to Fort Dodge. He was sorry and a little miffed his mother had waited so long to pass on the message. I told Gary it was fine, and he didn't need to worry about it. The temperature outside was about twenty degrees, which was normal for early morning temperatures in late October. My only option on such late notice was to use my motorcycle. I went out to the garage and pulled out my 1973 Honda 350 four-cylinder. I put on my coat and gloves and knew it would be a miracle if the bike started.

I didn't have much gas, so I put it on reserve until I could get to the gas station. I swung my leg over the top, sat on the seat, pulled out the choke, and prayed, "God, help this thing to start." I waited a moment, pushed the start button, and nothing happened. I had a sinking feeling: the battery was dead. Then I remembered the kick start, so I bent over, pulled out the kick start and put my foot on it; and after lifting myself up, I came down with all my weight. To my relief, it started. I let the engine warm up a bit, and after a few minutes, I was headed down the road to the gas station, glad to be on my way. About five miles down the road, my hands were getting cold, and my eyes were watering, causing tears to stream down my face.

When I came to the next town, I stopped at the local convenience store on the highway and bought a pair of gloves and stood inside to warm up for the next few minutes. Soon, I was on my way again. I didn't let the cold bother me because I was looking forward to meeting Pam and Nancy's family. About twenty more miles down the road, I felt chilled to the bone. When I came to the next convenience store, I stopped and bought another pair of gloves and warmed up a bit, although it didn't help much. By this time, I was counting the miles, and my body temperature continued dropping. Finally, I reached Fort Dodge but was still about fifteen minutes away from my destination. While in Fort Dodge, I stopped at yet another convenience store and bought another pair of gloves. It was the fourth pair, and my hands had grown monstrous with the multiple layers. I looked rather silly with big hands and frozen tears sledding down my face. Initially, I didn't think I would suffer that much riding there on my motorcycle, but not having a windshield to block the wind made it a lot worse than riding a snowmobile in the middle of winter.

Finally I crested the last hill, and on the right a big, white farmhouse came into view. I rolled up the long lane and stopped on the west side of the house. I was so cold I couldn't walk in a straight line. I made my way to the back door and pushed the doorbell with my frozen finger on a hand that was still shaped like handle grips. After a minute or so, I heard the door opening on the inside of the porch. Nancy appeared and I could barely make her out because my vision was so blurred. She saw my face and said, "Are you okay?" Seeing the tears in my eyes, she thought I was crying. With my face frozen solid, I couldn't even talk straight, so I just nodded. She started laughing and said, "Come on in here and get warm." I was never so happy to see the inside of a house. Stepping in I immediately felt the warmth of the air, but I also felt the spirit of the house. There was peace filling the house. This was the first time I had experienced this—being in someone's house and sensing the spirit of God.

What a welcoming sight and sensation, coming to a house that was so warm and inviting and filled with genuine God-fearing people. Once we were inside the door, Nancy began to introduce her mother and little sister. She said her sister Pam and her father were both working and would be back later. They offered me something warm to drink, which I gladly accepted. While sitting there drinking a hot chocolate, I told them about my journey to Clare in the cold. Needless to say, it was so funny they could barely talk because they were laughing themselves silly. Eventually, they felt sorry for me and offered a hot bath so I could warm up my bones. I declined but later wished I had taken them up on the offer since it wasn't until the next day that I had full feeling back in my fingers and knees.

We spent the rest of the afternoon getting to know one another, telling stories, laughing, and talking about the good things God had done. It was a beautiful start to an enjoyable weekend. I had a feeling this was just the beginning of something really good. By this time, Pam and Nancy's father, Virlin, had come home from work. After introductions we talked until it was time to get Pam from work. Later we drove into town to pick up Pam, and we had dinner in Fort Dodge. On returning back at the farm place, we all sat down and continued to talk about the things Jesus was doing in all our lives. Since it was so cold out, they invited me to stay in the guest room for the night. I gladly accepted, looking forward to spending more time with my new Christian friends.

I lay down on the bed and looked up toward heaven, thanking God I had gotten there safely and for the new relationships. I woke up in the early morning with an overwhelming feeling that God was going to do something good. I was lying in my bed staring at the ceiling, trying to listen to the Holy Spirit and thanking God. All of a sudden, I felt as if I should ask Pam what her dream or vision was. I thought this was a little too early to be getting this personal, but at the same time, I felt at peace. I sort of hoped when I sat down for breakfast I would have forgotten what the Lord was asking me to do.

However, as I was getting ready for the day, the inclinations were not leaving but were getting stronger. Then I started making deals with the Lord. "Lord, if this is from you, when I sit down for breakfast, if Pam is there, then I will ask her the question." Well, I guess nothing is too hard for the Lord. After a hot shower and getting dressed, I looked into the kitchen, and only Nancy was there. I sat down, and she offered me a bowl of cereal. I thought, *I'll just ask Nancy if Pam has had a vision or dream.* So I went ahead and asked her, "Nancy, has Pam had any dreams or visions lately?"

"I don't know. Why don't you ask her," she said. Then she left the table and went upstairs while I was sitting there finishing my breakfast. Within a minute or so, Pam came into the kitchen and greeted me. She then prepared her own breakfast and sat down across from me.

After a few moments of silence in which I tried to muster up the nerve to ask her about what God had said to me that morning, over the sound of my own heartbeat, I blurted out, "Pam, has God shown you any visions or dreams lately?" She sat there silent, munching her cereal. I could tell thoughts were racing through her head, and I mentally kicked myself. *Oh boy, you've done it now. Time to grab your motorcycle keys and make your way out the door.* The silence seemed to go on forever, but, in reality, it was probably only half a minute. Finally, she looked up at me and told me she would not tell anyone what God had shown her. I could tell what she was thinking, so I took her hand and said, "It's okay. Do whatever you want to do."

She began to describe a time when she had finished praying but desired to be still before the Lord. She had fallen into a half-sleep. She could hear a record playing and her family's voices in the house, but she couldn't make out the words. Then she said, "I saw a beautiful scene. Two people were walking together hand in hand. If love were visible, you could have seen it, and you knew these two loved the Lord. It was natural. Then they came up over the crest of a hill arm in arm. Love was radiating off their faces. They loved each other, and they loved the Lord." She said, "I woke up and said, 'Lord, I was supposed to be listening to you, and I went to sleep. That was so beautiful! What does that mean?' I felt the Lord say, 'One of those people is you.'"

Then I said to Pam, "I'm the other person. I just now saw the picture you described. This morning the Lord impressed on me to ask you what your vision was." It was at this time that Pam and I knew we were going to get married. What we were feeling at that moment was surreal. As we gazed at each other, Pam had tears running down her cheeks. We were amazed at what the Lord had done. This was great news for us, but for her parents, this would be shocking. Pam's parents were raised traditional Lutherans in the Missouri Synod church and had just recently been exposed to the charismatic movement.

I told Pam that I would not marry her without her father's blessing, and I felt like Jesus would honor this request because of the circumstances. If this was of God, then God needed to confirm it. Her parents didn't know me, and I understood how they would naturally feel in this situation. I wasn't about to start a relationship with Pam, or them, on the wrong foot. If this was going to be a long-term relationship, it was important to do things right and have the Lord's blessing. I didn't want to start a relationship because I was needy or felt the desire to have someone in my life. When I was in charge of my own life, before I surrendered to Jesus, I made a lot of mistakes in relationships; and I wasn't about to start this relationship without Jesus being in the middle of it. Common sense and God's Word told me that the person one marries is important because of the commitment involved: "The two shall become one flesh" (Genesis 2:24).

Marriage is a contract of cooperation and should not be looked at lightly. We make decisions together, play together, work together, and build a life with a family. God designed marriage to be a representation of how Christ loved the church and gave himself up for it. Ephesians 5:25 states, "Husbands love your wives, just as Christ loved the church and gave himself up for her." Marriage is not based on a fairytale emotion or infatuation. Of course, infatuation is a real emotion, but marriage is not to be based on feelings.

What a weekend! The Lord was working in such a personal and intimate way in my life and in the lives of others. We are often deceived in thinking that Jesus is not concerned about the details of our lives. God has to know everything or he wouldn't be God.

Psalm 139:1–10 states:

> You have searched me and you know me. You know when
> I sit and when I rise; you perceive my thoughts from afar.

You discern my going out and my lying down; you are familiar with all my ways. Before a word is on my tongue you know it completely, O Lord. You hem me in behind and before; you have laid your hand upon me. Such knowledge is too wonderful for me, too lofty for me to attain. Where can I go from your Spirit? Where can I flee from your presence? If I go to the heavens, you are there; if I make my bed in the depths, you are there. If I rise on the wings of the dawn, if I settle on the far side of the sea, even there your hand will guide me; your right hand will hold me fast.

The times we stumble in life are when we think he is not concerned for us personally and we feel we must earn a good standing with him before he will bless us. This is a lie of the enemy. Romans 5:8 says, "But God demonstrates his own love for us in this: While we were still sinners, Christ died for us." All we have to do is surrender our lives to him. It's not about us; it's about him and his kingdom.

It was Sunday, and the weekend was winding down. I told Pam I felt like Jesus told me I would leave for home when her father put his hands on us and prayed a blessing. Later that afternoon, Virlin walked into the fireplace room where we were all seated. He said he wanted to bless us before I left. He laid his hands on Pam and me and blessed us. The prayer of blessing happened exactly how the Lord had shown it to me. This was my okay to start for home.

WRESTLE WITH GOD

I T WAS TIME to go home. Fortunately, the temperature was in the seventies. I rode up the lane out to the county blacktop. A southern breeze warmed me as I headed east. I could see dried corn leaves blowing across the road. It was so different from the ride just a few days ago. A lot had transpired since that ride, and I had many reasons to be thankful. God had shown me he wanted to be intimately involved in my life. When I arrived home, I went up to my one-room apartment and began to thank God for the things he had done over the weekend; I was totally blown away.

At the same time, I thought, *Am I ready for this?* I had a small argument with Jesus in which I told him that a relationship with him was enough for me. I didn't feel like I needed a relationship with a woman. After a short silence, he calmed me with these words, "You need help." This showed me that I was not dependent on people for emotionally-based relationships, which was a huge sign of growth to me. It also led me to pray and ask God for confirmation of what he was doing.

The Lord showed me later that people need to be married to him first so their own marriages will be balanced and stable.

With school going on, Pam and I could only see each other about once a month. Pam was in her senior year of high school and was working toward becoming the valedictorian of her class, so she didn't need my distractions to deter her from achieving a high grade point average. We wrote letters to stay in touch. Pam and I were young and knew we were supposed to be together. We knew this was going to be God's plan because of our circumstances. This was the start of our love story.

THE MOVE
AND JOSEPH STORY

I T WAS MIDTERM. My cash funds were running low, and I needed to find a job to pay some bills. At the same time, the Lord was leading me in another direction regarding my education. I felt maybe he wanted me to attend Bible College for some formal education in theology, but I had no idea what to do or where to go. I took these matters to God.

During my first visit to Fort Dodge, I met Nancy's friend Steve. I told him everything I was going through and how I wanted to take a semester off. He invited me to come to Fort Dodge and live with him until I could hash things out. Taking him up on his offer, I moved in within a couple of weeks. He lived in a little one-and-a-half-story brick house. It was an upstairs apartment, which was especially small. We were guys, so we didn't need much space. He worked as a baker, so he spent his days sleeping. I had a lot of time to myself. I would pray, read, and search the Scriptures as he slept. While living together, we became pretty good friends.

One fall evening, I was sitting at the kitchen table making my way through the book of Genesis. I was reading about all the patriarchs, but one story really stuck out to me—the story of Joseph. The Holy Spirit was attaching me to this story as if I were reading about my own life. I read about all the hardships and difficulties he had and how he remained faithful and kept his eyes on the big picture. God bailed him out, saved him, and promoted him when the time was right. It was easy to relate to him and recognize the impact forgiveness made in his life. God used Joseph's difficult situations for his instruction but also to get him into a position to bless his family and the future nation of Israel.

By the time I had finished reading the story of Joseph, I felt cleansing tears streaming from my eyes. God was healing me of my emotional hurt and pain and disappointments. I strongly sensed the Holy Spirit say my life would be like Joseph's, and I would have to suffer hardships to learn the lessons the Holy Spirit wanted to teach me. He encouraged me to keep my eyes focused on the big picture not on the small fixations. God touched me so strongly that I could no longer sit in the chair at the table. I lay out on the floor weeping like a baby for more than an hour. When I arose from the floor and went to my bed, I was still weeping. I will never forget those moments.

PRAYING FOR CONFIRMATION

I WAS LIVING in Fort Dodge, much closer geographically to Pam and her family. They lived outside of the little town of Clare, Iowa, which was just northwest of Fort Dodge. Now instead of being over an hour away, I was only fifteen minutes away. Visits to their house were more frequent. We still prayed God would confirm our marriage at the appropriate time. Eventually, Pam told her parents what the Lord had shown us on that Sunday morning. We knew this would not be easy, as one might expect. They didn't know anything about me. When parents spend eighteen years or so investing into the lives of their children, they don't want a stranger coming along to destroy that investment. But Pam and I decided that it was time to tell everyone what God had shown us. Pam's mother had a difficult time with the news and told Pam, "This would be so much easier for me if a complete stranger came to our door and said God told you to marry Chuck." I agreed with her in this statement; it would be better for all of us.

I had been in Fort Dodge for almost three months when I felt I was supposed to fast and pray. I didn't know for how long, but I had things on my mind to set before the Lord. This was the first time I had decided to fast any meal, so this was a big deal for me. I didn't know how I would respond or feel; all I knew was that I desired to lay out the things on my heart before the Lord—one of which was the marriage time confirmation. In a previous prayer time, the Lord shared with me the date of our marriage—June 21, 1979. After the Lord showed me this date, he reminded me of a time in high school when I was in study hall. A few of us guys were sitting around talking about the day we would like to get married. I remember saying the day I would like to get married would be June 21. It was amazing how the Lord had brought that back to my memory. I had said this before I was a Christian and before I had any idea about God or Jesus. It just proved, once again, how intimate God is. He knows everything.

So, I began the fast. I reminded myself my hunger should call me to pray, and it did. I couldn't sit around to eat right now, so I had to focus. (It was difficult to refuse lunch invitations.) Steve was fasting with me, so it was easier to hold each other accountable. We spent time praying together and separately. In my prayer time, I asked the Lord to confirm his word in my life. I didn't want people to believe me just because I said the Lord was showing me the date of our marriage. I wanted him to confirm it and bring peace to the idea of marriage to Pam.

Marriage is a big deal, and I did not consider it lightly. I had to know for sure. The Lord knew I had to be certain because I had screwed up so many times before. This went on for four days; and on the fourth day, a friend of ours called Steve and me and invited us over for a spaghetti supper. We told them we would call them back with an answer. So when we got off the phone, we prayed together and felt a release from the fast. We accepted the invitation for a delicious spaghetti dinner. To my surprise, my stomach had shrunk, and I could not eat very much at all. I was stuffed to the gills. It was a satisfying way to end a fast.

A few weeks later, Pam and I attended a New Year's Eve retreat with my youth group. We had a lot of fun together. I had the opportunity to introduce Pam to some of my Christian friends. While we were there, we had some free time to pray together. It was during that prayer time Pam told me she felt as if the Lord had told her the date of June 21 for our marriage. I'm sure she assumed it was June 21 in a later year. She confessed to me that if it were 1979, it would be a miracle. The plans would have to be put together quickly.

It was January in Iowa, and there were reports of an approaching snowstorm. Because of the storm, Steve and I had to spend the weekend in Fort Dodge. We were disappointed we would not be able to see the girls. Friday night the snow began to fall. On Sunday, after the storm had blown over, I got a call from a very excited Pam. "Something really neat has happened this weekend, and you have to come out here as soon as you can." I had no idea what had transpired. I thought maybe someone had struck it rich or Pam had received a scholarship for college. Needless to say, the drive out to the farmhouse was full of anticipation. As I was looking down at the seat to undo my seatbelt and pick up my gloves, Pam's mother came running up to the car and asked me with tears in her eyes and a smile on her face, "What date did God say you were supposed to get married?"

I said, "I don't know if this is a good time to tell you."

She replied, "It's okay, just tell me."

So, I ventured, "Well, June 21, 1979."

She hugged me. "Oh! This is so exciting! I can't believe this is happening."

"What do you mean? What is happening?" I asked.

She said, "This is so wonderful. Just come in the house, and we will explain it to you."

Was God already confirming his word? I stepped into the house where everyone was smiling and excited. As I stood in the kitchen, everyone came out to greet me. There were three visitors who were complete strangers. Pam introduced me to Mike Foley.

She told me this story: "Mike attends Concordia College in Nebraska. He came to the house as a representative of his college to raise money for the new library they were planning to build on campus. They were meeting with church members and giving presentations of the school's needs.

"When Mike arrived it had started snowing. With it being so close to supper time, my mother invited him to stay for the meal and give his presentation to the family after supper. On the center of the kitchen table was Mom's Bible with a *Charismatic Renewal* newsletter lying underneath it. Mike accepted the invitation for dinner and noticed the newsletter. He asked my mom if she were Charismatic.

Mom affirmed that she was, and Mike said, 'Praise God. So am I!'

"After dinner, we talked and Mike and Dad each took time to share how being filled with the Holy Spirit had changed their lives.

"Sometime later Mike went to start his car, but it wouldn't start. The snow was getting deeper, but it was not extremely cold yet, so he couldn't figure out why the car wouldn't start. Then Dad joined him, and they worked on the car, but to no avail. The storm was getting worse. As a result, my parents suggested Mike stay overnight until the snowstorm was over. So the decision was made that he would stay the night.

"Mike came to Iowa with two other friends from college who were at different locations. The next day he called to inform them he was having car problems, so they both came to our farm. (You met Mike's friends, both named Jeff.) The wind picked up, and it started snowing again, turning into blizzard-like conditions. My dad and all three guys went outside to make another attempt at starting Mike's car before conditions worsened. After many attempts, they all came inside and announced that now all three cars would not start. We all felt it was strange that all the cars wouldn't start when it wasn't extremely cold. Since the storm worsened, there was no other choice but to stay the night. Now instead of one college guy stranded at our house, there were three. With more snow on the way, there wasn't much else to do but enjoy each other's company."

Pam continued her story: "That afternoon, Nancy, the three guys, and I went into the living room to hang out. I started hemming a dress, and Mike stretched out on the floor to relax. After a pause in the conversation, Mike said, 'June 21. Jeff, is that your birthday?' Well, Jeff said, 'No.'"

When I heard what Mike had asked Jeff, my heart almost jumped out of my chest. I wanted to blurt out, *What do you mean by that question, Mike?* But I just kept quiet.

Pam went on: "We ate dinner and had a good time laughing and telling stories. After dinner the whole family and our three stranded guests found a place in the living room. Mike began to share, through a word of knowledge, many of the details and events of our family during the last two months. [A word of knowledge is one of the gifts of the Holy Spirit listed in 1 Corinthians 12:7–11.] After describing what the Lord was showing him, Mike asked me, 'Pam, are you getting married? Last night, when I was going to bed, I felt the Lord saying to me the word *confirmation*. I kept hearing it so strongly that I wrote it here on the inside cover of my Bible.' Mike opened up his Bible and showed everyone where he had written the word *confirmation*. All day he asked the Lord what it could all mean."

Pam then reported Mike's startling words: "Today when we were in the living room together and I was lying on the floor, it was as if I saw a neon sign in front of me. The sign was flashing June 21, 1979… wedding. Pam, I knew you needed to hear that."

Pam took a breath. "I was so excited and told Mike that June 21st was the day the Lord showed us we were to get married. I revealed to him that we had been praying that God would bring confirmation so everyone would be at peace with what God was showing us to do. I told him we wanted clarity so people wouldn't doubt and wonder if this were some emotional whim. Chuck, Mike told me the Lord told him that this day would be a day of healing and unity."

With awe and excitement, she finished her story: "God sent confirmation of our marriage on January 13, 1979, and we should start making plans to be wed on June 21, 1979."

I couldn't believe what I was hearing; it was like music to my ears—a dream come true. God heard my prayers, and he had answered them. I began to trust God was speaking to me, and he was leading me in a very specific way. What a marriage story he had given us! I could always look back at this and say, "This was meant to be." There is no doubt God was in our marriage. The event of this confirmation silenced all the doubts in us and in our families. I think it would be right to mention how the Lord sent a snowstorm to keep me isolated in Fort Dodge that weekend and away from being involved in this confirmation in any way. It could not be said that I influenced anyone's thinking to bring about this confirmation.

Jesus knew what it would take to keep me out of the mix, and he was big enough to arrange the circumstances. This is a reminder that when we do things God's way and in God's time, he works out all the details. Jesus is moved when we are moved to seek him with our whole heart. He wants first things first; then all the small details will fall into place.

LET THE PLANNING BEGIN

P AM AND I began the planning stages of our wedding. It was my idea to have an outdoor wedding because there's no better sanctuary than the one Jesus made, and Pam agreed. Her grandparents lived in a white house on a farm about a mile and a half from her parents' home. They had a pasture on the north side of their house surrounded by mature burr oak trees; it was a beautiful setting. We spoke with everyone involved in the events of that weekend, and they thought it was a great idea—an outdoor wedding on the old farm. How romantic! Pam is an organizer, so she took care of the little details. One thing we did decide together about was how we would have the invitations written. We believed so strongly that we wanted an outdoor wedding and that God was going to bless it, that we left off the words "alternative indoor location in case of inclement weather." The other unique thing about our wedding day was that June 21, 1979, fell on a Thursday. I'm sure this caused scheduling conflicts for some people, but we put it into the hands of the Lord to bring the people he wanted there for our special day.

We knew for sure we were to get married, and everyone was at peace with the decision, especially Pam's parents. While Pam worked on wedding details, I began to work on getting a car and a wedding ring. All I had at the time was a motorcycle. I told the Lord I needed to sell the motorcycle and get a car. The days were getting warmer, so I decided to get my motorcycle ready to be sold. I had been keeping the motorcycle in the back room of an old storefront in a little town outside of Fort Dodge. It was a warm day when I arrived at the storefront. I walked into the back room where my bike was. Then I opened up the garage door to let in some air and light, so I could work on my motorcycle and get it ready to sell. This little 350 four-cylinder Honda was a really clean bike. While polishing the fender, I noticed a shadow standing near the overhead door. I looked over and saw a young man about my age. "Can I help you?" I asked.

He pointed. "That really looks like a nice bike."

"Yeah, I am just getting it ready to sell. I'm getting married this June."

"My friend is looking for a motorcycle just like this one. How much do you want for it?" he asked.

"$850."

"Can you wait until tomorrow and hold the bike for me?"

"Sure," I said.

Then he shook my hand. "I'll be back tomorrow with the cash."

I turned in utter amazement looked up and said to the Lord, "You are amazing!" The next day, just as he had said, the same guy showed up with his friend and $850 in cash to buy the motorcycle. I hardly said a word to promote the sale. As soon as they looked at it, they knew they wanted it. He handed me the cash, and I gave him the signed title. He asked me where the choke was, sat on the motorcycle, and held out his hand for the keys. I couldn't believe how fast it all happened. I was so blessed by the Lord's handiwork in my life. To me, this was another confirmation that the Lord was working out all the details for the marriage.

I told the Lord I needed a decent car and a wedding car and a wedding ring. That $850 wouldn't go very far. Finding a good car at that price wouldn't be easy, so I asked him for ideas on what to do. At the time, I was working for a local tree cutter to help pay bills. Running the boom truck at work one day, I remembered my friend back in college, Gary Beer, who had a car for sale—a German-made Opel. Gary was a good friend of mine, and we both had become Christians around the same time.

I called Gary and asked him if he still had his car for sale, and he did. He wanted about $500 for it, so I bought it. I also knew I needed a best man for my wedding, so I decided at that time I would ask Gary if he wanted to be my best man. We had shared so much together, and I wanted my wedding party to be believers. I told him the wedding was on June 21, 1979. "Wow, so soon," he said. "I didn't even know you had a girlfriend." I laughed and said that I would be coming to Iowa Falls in a couple of weeks and would stop by and pay for the car.

When I showed up at his house, he pulled the car out of the garage and told me, "Since you're getting married, I thought I would sell you the car for $400, and that would be my wedding present to you." I thanked him for helping me out and gave him the $400. Since I had a car, I could take the extra money and apply it to the purchase of a wedding ring for Pam. Once again, the Lord proved himself as my provider.

Time was passing, and I was thinking about our future and where I wanted to go to school. I had been studying art illustration in college and was looking toward getting a fine arts degree. But as my faith was growing, I felt the Lord leading me in other directions for education. A couple of my friends talked to me about the Bible College they were attending in Des Moines, Open Bible College. Every time I heard about it, I was intrigued. It was the only Christian college I knew about in the area because I knew very little about formal Christianity or Christian colleges. I didn't know that this was a Pentecostal college or what Pentecostal meant. There was something inside of me that knew this just might be the college for me. Since we were preoccupied with wedding planning, I never discussed with Pam my intentions for the fall or anything about attending Open Bible College.

One evening, Pam and I were in her front yard talking over future plans, and I was listening to her talk about where she wanted to go to school. Knowing nothing of her college plans before we met, I was stunned when she told me she wanted to go to a college in Des Moines, Open Bible College. Wow, can you believe it? She was thinking of going to the very same college I felt like the Lord was leading me to attend. Talk about God working out all the details! I told her that was the very same college I was planning on attending in the fall. She and I were both amazed God had put it in our hearts to attend the same college even before we met each other. From that time on, we made plans to attend Open Bible College in Des Moines, Iowa.

June was quickly approaching; and as plans were unfolding, Pam was making her own wedding dress, which was a huge task. I was marrying a very talented and intelligent person who feared God. She was working on all these details, and she had not yet graduated from high school. The first thing she had to do before the wedding day was to get through her high school graduation. Pam worked hard in school and was valedictorian of her class. I was very proud of her. I have always believed that my wife could have easily been a doctor or a lawyer, but she informed me she was not interested in a career. She wanted to raise a family and invest her time in taking care of our children and being my wife.

That was just fine with me. My thinking was being transformed. I was no longer single; from now on, I needed to be aware of the needs of another person. I had to think of Pam and what was best for us—not just for me. We arranged to live in Iowa Falls until the fall semester of college.

THE WEDDING

O N JUNE 20, the day before the wedding, I was still in Iowa Falls. I woke up and poked my head out the door. The wind was blowing about forty miles an hour. I began my drive to Pam's grandparents' house to set up for the wedding, not realizing how the wind might affect all our arrangements. Somewhere along Highway 20, the car I'd bought from Gary blew off a radiator hose and dumped all the engine coolant on the highway. The coolant light flashed on, and I was forced to pull over and stop the car right next to a farmhouse. I pushed the car into the driveway and approached the house to ask the owners if I could borrow a screwdriver to put the hose back on the radiator.

When I knocked on the door, a timid woman cracked the door slowly and acted a little afraid of me. I told her my car broke down, and I asked if I could borrow a screwdriver. Fortunately, she had one which she lent to me reluctantly. I thanked her and went right to work putting the hose back on. After the hose was on, I had to wait for the engine to cool a bit. While waiting, I sat facing south feeling the wind blow by me and enjoying the presence of the Lord.

I wasn't worked up about all this the day before my wedding, which was a little unusual for me. In a circumstance like this, I would normally have grown anxious about getting everything fixed. I felt the comfort and peace of the Lord on me, and I knew everything was going to be all right. I really wasn't even thinking about how the wind could affect our outdoor wedding. It was a memorable time for me. Within a short amount of time, I had water back in the engine. I gave the screwdriver back to the lady, thanked her for her help, and was back on the road again.

When I finally arrived, the work was already under way. Pam's folks and all her sisters were busy making preparations for the big day. We began to set up the hay bales to support the 2 × 12s that would be used for guest seating for our outdoor ceremony. Together we prayed that the wind would die down before tomorrow and everything would go according to plan. People milled around completing their assigned tasks, and it was a wonderful feeling having all this help. I could sense the Lord's help in everything that was being done; he was working out all the details and doing things behind the scenes to set up the day he had planned for us. The strong winds stopped at 6:00 p.m.

The next day, I woke up to the music of birds singing their songs of thanksgiving. There was a still peace in the air that morning. *Praise the Lord. Jesus has given us a calm, cloudless day with no wind.* We spent the rest of the day tying up loose ends, setting up the arbor, getting the musical equipment and PA system set up, and arranging the rest of the hay bales for the seating. Pam's dad had a sprayer he put on the back of his tractor. He put water in the tank to spray down the lane to keep the dust down. There wasn't a cloud in the sky. It was a perfect day, the first day of summer, and the day I was getting married.

The wedding ceremony was scheduled for 6:00 p.m., and Pam and I had requested two ministers to perform the ceremony. One minister was a Lutheran minister from the church Pam's family attended in their township. The other minister was from the Epworth Methodist church in Fort Dodge where we first met on the lay witness mission. His name was Pastor Robert McCannon. We really fell in love with Pastor McCannon while we were in his church for the mission. He loved God, and that love was very visible on this man's face.

Pam had asked her sisters and a close Christian friend to be bridesmaids and her sister Nancy to be her maid of honor. I wanted my closest Christian brothers to be my groomsmen. Gary Beer was my best man. I wore a white tuxedo with tails, and the groomsmen wore light blue tuxedos. The wedding hour was upon us, and we were all ready to begin the service. We had invited our friends and family and also had the pleasure of having our honored guest, Mike Foley, present with us. He was the one who had brought the word of confirmation for our wedding back in January. Pam and I were grateful to Mike and to the Lord for what had happened, and everyone was still in awe because of the Lord's goodness to us. The day was beautiful. Jesus was fulfilling what he said he would do today. The sun was shining bright; there was a slight breeze to keep us all cool for the first day of summer. It was gorgeous.

The processional music began, and the wedding party got into position. My groomsmen and I prepared to walk up the middle aisle. I asked my best man if he had the ring, and he started patting all his pockets with a look of concern on his face, causing everyone to laugh. As we started walking up front, we could sense the peace and joy of the Lord everywhere. The song by Ted Sandquist "O Come Let Us Worship" started, and my bride was at the center aisle beaming with the joy of the Lord. All of her attendants awaited her arrival at the front. Pam began her approach with her mom and dad as her escorts. Their faces radiated the blessing of the day. The formalities of giving the bride away were completed in the normal tradition with a few tears and hugs.

When Pam was finally presented to me, we both looked at each other joyously trembling—almost surreal. I kept thinking, *Is this day really happening*? The minster began the ceremony explaining the definition of marriage. I was nervous and don't recall much of what was said. Pam and I kept looking into each other's eyes. The very moment in time God had planned for us was here. After the minister's statements came the time to recite our vows. We had taken some time before the wedding day to write our own vows, and we both tried to memorize them to keep from faltering when the time came. It didn't help; we both stumbled in our recitations. Despite having a strong sense of God's presence, we were overcome with our own emotions and nervousness. It reminded me of the fact that we were not perfect, but that God's enabling power was able to work in us even though we weren't perfect.

We made it through the vows without mishap, and now it was time to kiss the bride. The minister said, "I now pronounce you man and wife," and I nervously took my new wife in my arms and gave her a modest but heartfelt kiss. Then Pastor McCannon said, "I present to you Mr. and Mrs. Charles Thomas." Now that's something I had never heard before.

At the end of the service, the wedding guests paraded up to the front so we could greet them and thank them for coming to share our special day. This was a remarkable, God-anointed time, and we heard a lot of unique comments. Most of the people said how they felt such peace and how they felt at home being there. One couple mentioned that they saw two doves in the trees that were singing during the ceremony. Another person mentioned they could smell the fragrance of flowers coming up over the hill. They said they walked over to the top of the hill to look at the flowers. There were none. They said it must be a miracle from heaven. The photographer told us that he had done many weddings in his career, but he had never been to a wedding where he felt the *man upstairs* was actually there. Because of that, he told us he wanted to take some pictures of us with the sun over our heads. His goal was to create a cross effect with the picture. It turned out wonderfully. When people came up to greet us, many had tears in their eyes and said they had never been to a wedding where they knew God was in attendance. We never prompted anyone to make such comments. I was blown away by the fact that our family and friends recognized that God's Spirit was in attendance.

Pam and I remarked later that we felt compassion for people while we were greeting them. There was definitely a spirit of healing and unity in our receiving line just as Mike Foley had said there would be back in January; it was amazing. All the words God spoke to us in January were coming to pass. Seeing God do what he said he would do on that day showed me how intimate and personal he is and how he loves to be with his children. What a memory he had given us, and another great story was added to our lives.

At the reception, we served the traditional multi-tiered cake. While people milled around, Pam and I continued to have photographs taken. It seemed as if the photographer was truly amazed and really wanted to do these pictures more than I did. I thought it was a little unusual because most photographers like to get the pictures taken and be on their way, but it almost seemed as if he was on a mission to inject a special blessing into the photographs. We hadn't asked him to go the extra mile, but he took it upon himself to take extra time and make it right. I felt as if God was orchestrating every event of the day.

Friends had filled my car completely full of crumpled newspapers and had dumped a couple of bags of rice inside. When it was time for Pam and me to leave, we found our car so full we couldn't see through the car windows. On the back window, someone wrote, "Chuckey's in love."

Pam and I were getting ready to leave. Pam was standing on the passenger side of the car, and I had the driver's side door open trying to pull out enough of the paper so we could see through the windows. What we didn't know was that my buddies had worked out a scheme. While I pulled out paper, a few of my groomsmen surrounded Pam. They grabbed her and began to carry her off. They were stealing my bride, and they were going to hide her. I heard her screams, and I dashed over and rescued her. I returned to my side of the car and frantically removed more of the news-paper. Once again, they made another attempt to steal her. This time, they got halfway to the escape car. Her screams alarmed me to the rescue. I became her Prince Charming that day to save her from their evil schemes. The guys finally gave up and surrendered to the fact that the Prince was going to win.

It took me quite some time to get the car cleaned out. Well, except for the rice. I guess I wasn't expecting their little tricks, but when I think about it, I shouldn't have been surprised that they had something planned. They were a bunch of fun-loving guys. I never did get all the rice out of that car. After all the fun was over, it was time for Pam and me to leave on our honeymoon. We had planned a three-day getaway to the Amana Colonies in Iowa. We had a wonderful time, but it was much too short. Real life was upon us.

As we had planned, we were going to school in the fall in Des Moines. The summer moved along quickly, and it wasn't long before we were loading a trailer full of our stuff for the move south. Pam's parents helped us move to married student housing on the campus of Open Bible College in Des Moines. There the Lord began to show me things in the Word of God, especially in my Old and New Testament survey classes. It was a time of instruction and learning.

BASKETBALL DREAM

OPEN BIBLE COLLEGE was a small college on the south side of Des Moines. They had a basketball team that traveled regionally for games and tournaments. I was encouraged by a few of my friends to go out for the team. I was reluctant to try out because I had no high school experience. Even though I didn't have a lot of formal experience with the game, I loved to play. After much coaxing from my friends, I decided to go out. It was always one of my desires to be able to play basketball for a real school even if the school was small. I didn't care; I just wanted to play to see what it was like. I always had a dream of winning a game in the last few seconds. This small school setting would at least give me a chance to try.

As a team, we traveled to Missouri and Nebraska for games and tournaments. Sometimes I would start in games, and in other games, I was the first guy off the bench. I particularly remember one home game against Vennard College. I hadn't started that game, and I was warming the far end of the bench—away from the coach. This particular game was close the whole way through, and some of our starters were getting into foul trouble. It was a little nerve-racking. With about seven seconds left in the game, we were down by one point, and one of our forwards fouled out. The coach looked down the bench and said, "Chuck, you're going in." I jumped up out of my seat and went over to the officials' table and signed in.

When the whistle blew for the ref to call me, I forgot to take off my warm-ups. I was excited. That's all I can say. We had the ball out of bounds below our own basket. I stood at the top of the key waiting for the inbound pass. A defensive man was in my face. I ran around him to the baseline right under the basket. My teammate passed me the ball, and I went up for a shot on the left side directly under the basket. Two Vennard Cougars collapsed on me defensively, and I drew a shooting foul with five seconds left in the game. Vennard called a time-out to try to ice me. *Is this really happening?* I had always wanted a chance to win a game in the last seconds. God was giving me what I had dreamed of.

During the time-out, the coach said, "Relax and make the shots." When the time-out was over, I headed to the free throw line. I dribbled the ball a couple of times, took a couple of deep breaths, and let the shot go. It went right through the net. The game was tied, and everybody was standing up, cheering and screaming at the top of their lungs. When I was single, I used to go up to the city park and shoot about one hundred free throws a night, not ever realizing I would have this opportunity. Vennard called a time-out after the made shot. During the time-out, our coach said, "Play good defense, but don't foul." Then he looked at me. "Chuck, you made one. Now make another one." I nodded and headed back out to the free throw line.

The referee handed me the ball and warned everybody about jumping in the lane too early. Again, I dribbled the ball a couple times, took another couple deep breaths, and aimed for the front of the rim. I let it go. When I released, I felt like it was going short, I started to lean forward, trying to keep my balance and keep from falling in the lane. Just before I made a step into the lane, the ball swooshed through the net, and the building erupted. I had made the shot, and we had a one point lead. Right away, Vennard had the ball out of bounds and was passing it in. Our defense hustled into their positions. Vennard ran up the court and took a shot, which hit the back of the rim and bounced in and out of the basket. We got the rebound as the time clock expired. Everybody started dancing around and yelling. We won the game, and Jesus had fulfilled one of the desires of my heart when I didn't even see it coming. I was totally amazed by his ability to shock me and fulfill something I thought would never happen. Dreams do come true!

GOOD DEFENSE

T O WIN GAMES in basketball, a team needs a good defense. In life we also need a good defense and understanding of Scripture to be successful. I desired in my young faith to have confirmation that what I believed was true. I was naïve to scriptural truth and how it applied to everyday life and needed to mature.

My off-campus job was working for Parachem Corporation. I worked in their warehouse, sending out shipments of leaf soap and repairing/replacing the leaf soap dispensers. While I was working there, they had a banner year and wanted to add someone else in the warehouse to help me do my job. I asked my college classmate Tom Clegg if he wanted a job working with me. Tom was hired. We spent many afternoons working together and practicing our defense of Scripture. Tom and I would present arguments concerning the validity of God and the Scriptures to one another and then would give scriptural evidence in defense. One of us would act as the devil's advocate, throwing out rebuttals to the truth. Whoever came up with the best answer won the argument. It made us think about our faith, where we stood, and how much we knew or didn't know the Scriptures. These styles of discussion led to many interesting afternoons together.

We were learning how to handle God's Word as Paul advised Timothy to do in 2 Timothy 2:15:

> Do your best to present yourself to God as one approved, a workman who does not need to be ashamed and who correctly handles the word of truth.

YOUTH PASTOR OR MECHANIC?

A FTER ONE YEAR at Open Bible College, Pam and I were approached by an Assemblies of God pastor from Fort Dodge who was looking for a youth pastor to help build a youth group. I felt the Lord's leading to go to Fort Dodge and be a youth pastor. So, at the end of the school year, we moved to an apartment in Fort Dodge. Pam and I were excited about the ministry opportunity. My responsibilities included hanging out with the youth, preaching, teaching, and helping them understand their faith.

This was an unpaid position, so I decided to continue my education in a hands-on trade. Since I was interested in auto mechanics, I enrolled at Iowa Central Community College in their two-year auto mechanics program. I also worked at the YMCA. Pam had a job in a local chiropractor's office. It was a difficult time for us financially, and the Lord stretched our faith and taught us to trust in him for our needs.

While serving as a youth pastor, I learned ministry can be difficult and requires a definite call from God to fulfill his purposes. I saw how God deals with people in his time. Young people are eager to see results, but they often discover that God takes a lifetime to help or change some people. I was a leader of a youth group and still a youth myself. I think this time was more about my own development as a minister of the gospel than anything else. Being a youth pastor, I learned to be a cheerleader and an encourager. I can remember times when I felt like things were out of control and I wasn't doing a good job; but at the same time, I felt as if Jesus was preparing me for the future. This was a time when he honed my character and my preaching to bring me to a new level of maturity.

While at Iowa Central, I had a chance to live my faith out loud. I talked to my classmates about my life of faith and what Jesus had done in me since I became a Christian. I met Lenny, whom I talked to as we worked together on our classwork. Lenny was a God-fearing person and had muscles galore. Since he was my school buddy, we spent a lot of time together talking about God, our existence, and why we were here on this earth.

One morning, he approached me and told me he had surrendered to Jesus and asked him to come into his life. This was the best news I had received all year. At times as a youth pastor, I was discouraged because I didn't see many changes in the lives of those in my youth group. When Lenny told me he became a Christian, it gave me confidence that God was working behind the scenes when I wasn't aware of it. Lenny and I had become good friends, and we were growing in our faith together. He started going to Bible studies in his hometown and would report back to me the good things he was learning. Watching him grow was a breath of fresh air and the encouragement I needed to keep moving forward.

Being a youth pastor, I sometimes found it difficult to be encouraged because of the challenges I faced each day. One day at school I went to my locker to get some illustrated gospel tracts to show Lenny. I had no intention of giving them to the other guys in my class. On my way back to my work area, guys began asking me what was in my hand. I was surprised that they were all approaching me and asking me for one of the tracts; it was a miracle. Lenny and I were shocked. Everyone was standing around reading the tracts. It was definitely a God thing.

SCHOOL CONFIRMATION

BEING STRETCHED IS difficult. Living in Fort Dodge was tough in many ways for us—especially financially. The Lord had small blessings for us, which kept us encouraged at just the right time. Yet it didn't make things any easier. We were approaching my graduation from auto mechanic school at Iowa Central, and I was seeking the Lord about where to go next.

One Sunday evening at church as I sat in the front, eyes closed, with people worshiping all around me, a strange sensation overcame me. I felt semiconscious of my surroundings as if I were floating in the air. I really wasn't praying at the time or doing anything in particular. I just remember sitting with Pam next to me and the youth group seated around us. In that moment, I got this overwhelming knowledge that God was calling me back to finish Bible College. This unique feeling stayed with me throughout the whole service. I was physically in the service, but I wasn't participating in what was going on around me. Thoughts of returning to

Bible College kept running through my head, and there was an overwhelming emotion of joy welling up within me.

I knew God was speaking to me. This had never happened to me before. I was ecstatic. I felt as if a ton of bricks was off my shoulders and that I had clear direction for what I was supposed to do next. I was beaming on the inside but hadn't yet disclosed this information to my wife. This would be the next hurdle, so I began praying immediately that God would finish his work toward this direction. Pam knew my graduation was coming up and that I could get a job as a mechanic to begin bringing in some income to make it easier for us to live instead of just scraping by. Her employment was paying our bills, and she was ready to transfer that responsibility to me.

Times were difficult financially, and we both wanted to be relieved of that burden. I wasn't ready for God to move me to Bible College and not be in unity with my wife, which was important to me for the health of our relationship. Once we arrived home from the service, I shared with Pam everything God had shown me, and she listened quietly. It was a little difficult to talk because I knew it might be upsetting to her. When I had finished telling her all the Lord had shared with me that evening, I think she felt numb. Then she said, "If this is God, then he needs to confirm it to us."

"I totally agree," I replied. So Pam and I began praying that the Lord would confirm his word to us.

A couple of months later, we were prayerfully preparing for a youth conference we were to be attending. We had been continually praying that God would confirm his word to us and use this conference to speak to our youth group. I knew that God would use the speakers to minister to all of us. The time arrived for us to attend the convention, so we loaded up the cars and made the short drive down to Ames. At the first evening service, a missionary from Brazil named Bernard Johnson spoke.

We had no idea who he was, but we were told he was like the Billy Graham of Brazil. Bernard was a fiery preacher. I don't remember much of what he said until he got to the end of his message. Pam had left the meeting to use the restroom, and when she arrived back into the convention center, she stood in the back of the large room. I was still sitting up front with the youth group. Bernard started using the gifts of the Holy Spirit and speaking things out in faith. Then through a word of knowledge and wisdom, he said, "There is a young man out here who has one year of Bible College and a couple of years of technical school, and you've been battling over whether or not you should go back to Bible school or go into the technical area in which you have been trained. The Lord says he wants you to go back to Bible College and finish getting your degree."

I was shocked. Jesus was doing it again. He was confirming his word to us and directing our steps. I looked to the back of the convention hall to see if I could see Pam. She was standing by the door, tears streaming down her face. In that moment, Jesus proved to me how much he cares and how much he wants to help us with our day-to-day decisions. Pam finally made it back to where we were sitting, and I asked her if she heard what Bernard just said. She quietly replied, "I heard every word." I knew I had heard God that Sunday night a few weeks earlier. And now my wife was on board with me. God worked out every detail.

BIBLE COLLEGE DREAM

SOMETIME LATER, AFTER we had told our family and close friends what the Lord was leading us to do, I had a dream. In this dream I saw tall oak trees in front of a building covered with windows, and to the right of the big building, I saw a circle drive entry. To the right of the driveway, I saw an ornate chapel building. During the dream, I felt a sense of peace and the comfort of home. I woke up and immediately told Pam what I had dreamt and said, "The college has a circle drive entry with a sign in front that says Central Bible College." I don't know why I was particularly drawn to this college, but I felt I should go there and check it out.

So in March, we scheduled a time to visit the campus. We had purchased a newer used car because we would be traveling more of a distance to get back and forth from school. When the day arrived for us to leave, it was raining wildly. It was the middle of March, and there were threats of tornadoes and severe thunderstorms on our trip. I figured it was just the distraction of the enemy. We agreed in prayer for safe travels before we left and started driving south out of Iowa.

It rained the whole way there. We drove for about nine hours, and there wasn't a dry piece of pavement the entire way. When we arrived in Springfield, Missouri, our close friends, Ed and Janet Harp, told us there were severe thunderstorms and tornadoes all the way through Missouri. I had a feeling that they would say that, but I did not have any fear about the trip. I knew Jesus had told us to go back to school, so I knew he would protect us and keep us from harm. We reached Springfield unscathed and thanked God for the enjoyable, though wet, trip.

We drove up to the entrance of Central Bible College campus. I noticed the circle drive and all the large oak trees that were in front of the administration building. It looked exactly like the image I had seen in my dream. In that moment, I knew this was the place I was supposed to be. This was before the days of the World Wide Web, so usually one wouldn't have a picture of a place in his mind before he had been there. This only made God's confirmation more miraculous. I had never seen this campus, so I knew my dream did not come from any previous picture. It was original—originally planted by God, who knew what the campus looked like. Amazing!

COLLEGE LIFE

O N THE DAY we arrived at Central Bible College, the business administrator of the college was showing us the apartment we were to move into. When he was giving us the tour, he asked me if I had a job. I told him I didn't, and he said, "If you want, you can work here. You can start Monday." This guy didn't know me, and he had already offered me a job. I had yet to unload the trailer. Needless to say, we were thankful.

The next Monday, I started my new job with the carpenter crew on campus. Pam started a temporary job selling light bulbs over the phone about a week after we arrived. God truly blessed her efforts there. When that job was completed, she found a job working for Sikes & Associates. This job was supposed to be temporary. It was a position in the office of Alford Sikes, who was the campaign manager for the Republican candidate for governor of Missouri, and who later would become the FCC chairman. When the campaign was over the job was supposed to end, but Al's wife, Marty, asked Pam to stay on after the campaign to assist with doing payroll for the five radio stations they owned. It was a good job for Pam, and it provided well for us.

In the midst of our studies and Pam's new job, we attended Park Crest Assembly of God church, a congregation on the south side of Springfield. One day we got a call from our friends from Iowa, Ed and Janet Harp, who were also attending Central Bible College. They had been giving seminary students rides to church, and they didn't know if they would be able to do it every time. They asked us if we would like to fill in when they weren't available. We gladly accepted. A few weeks later, we received a call asking if we would pick up someone from the seminary, a young man named David Balasingh.

When we arrived at the seminary, David was waiting on the sidewalk outside his apartment. We were running a little late, so after quick introductions, we were off to church. We found David to be very sincere about his faith. He told us the intimate details of what the Lord was doing in his life and the things he was learning and the people he was influencing. This first meeting would begin a lifelong friendship.

I spent the next three years finishing my degree. A degree can clear paths for opportunity, but a man's character and gifts keep him established. I knew getting a degree at college would open doors, but I also knew that the character God was developing in me (and the people I would meet) would influence the future ministry that God was working in me.

About a month before graduation, I started taking time every day to go out to the backwoods on campus and pray, seeking God's will about where we should go next. My favorite spot was on the side of a hill where the flat area of a rock stuck out. It was just large enough for me to lie on. It was also away from the campus activities, so I wasn't bothered much. It was a great time for me to be alone and focus on what was next on God's agenda for me. Jesus definitely knew how earnestly I wanted him to be involved in what was ahead. I had two opportunities of ministry.

One was to interview for a ministry position as the youth pastor in an Assemblies of God church in Naples, Florida. The other was a job working as a live-in counselor at Teen Challenge of the Midlands in Omaha, Nebraska.

I decided to take the Teen Challenge job. The people who told us about the opening were good friends of ours. We had met Larry and Sue Nelson while attending Open Bible College, and Larry and I talked many times about world situations and the things of God. This particular Teen Challenge was a women's center, so it was a requirement that Pam and I would work together. Pam and I prayed about the job and felt this was the way God was directing us. We would be starting in June.

It was finally the week of my graduation. What a relief; I thought I would never get my degree. I was so thankful he gave me the diligence to finish. I couldn't have done it without the help of my wife and Jesus leading us there. After I wrote my papers by hand, Pam helped me by typing them, preparing meals, and working to help pay the bills. My job on campus paid for my tuition, and I had gotten some help from the government.

I graduated college debt-free. Praise the Lord for his provision. That final week I was floating on cloud nine and felt completely relieved: all my work was done...thank God.

Pam and I met many people at CBC who taught us important things about the fundamentals of our faith such as prayer, fasting, Christian character, and studying God's Word. Bible College also gave me background knowledge about the writers of the Bible and the cultural implications that influenced the writing of that day. This helped us students understand why it was written and also how the Scripture applies to us today.

Attending a Bible College isn't any more spiritual than going to a secular college. One will encounter the same spectrum of people found anywhere else in the world, but there is a larger core of people who are focused on God's purpose for their lives. I had the choice of associating with those who were not seeking God or to associate with those who were. All of us have this choice every day, regardless of whether we're in a Bible College or not. I wanted more of God in my life, so I chose to be around people who would help me to grow into maturity and challenge me in my relationship with God.

TEEN CHALLENGE

A FTER TAKING A vacation in Florida, it was time to start packing up our things again. Everything we owned fit into a 4 × 8 U-Haul trailer. Pam and I were anticipating starting our new jobs at Teen Challenge and couldn't wait to head to Omaha to get things underway. It was about an eight-hour drive to Omaha, Nebraska, from Springfield, Missouri, and because of our anticipation, the drive seemed longer. We finally arrived at the white, three-story mansion. Our good friends from Open Bible College, Larry and Sue Nelson, saw us coming up the driveway and streamed out the front door to meet us. We hadn't seen each other for a couple of years.

Larry and Sue loved God. The compassion of the Lord was in their lives and evident on their faces. It was a blessed greeting after a long drive, and it gave me confidence that we had made the right decision to come to Teen Challenge. Larry asked us if we wanted the nickel tour. The house was huge, but as we walked closer, I noticed that it was in ill repair. The wide front porch was bigger than the apartment we'd just moved from, but the siding and paint were coming off. The eaves were rotting, there were a few broken storm windows, and the roof looked like it was leaking in several places.

While we were standing on the porch, I looked over to my left in the front yard and saw a faded yellow sign with the words "Teen Challenge of the Midlands" hand-painted in faded black paint. I had a sinking feeling that this house needed a lot of work to keep bad things from getting worse. And frankly, the appearance was a little embarrassing. If I had to guess, the house was approximately 6,000 sq. ft., and that would be a conservative estimate. The front porch had two picture windows on either side of the solid oak main entry door. Just inside the door was an oak-paneled foyer. The foyer sidelights were made of beveled glass. This house was too beautiful to go to waste and needed repair for the sake of the ministry.

After walking through the foyer, we entered into an open atrium with a grand stairway leading up to the second floor. The view was nothing short of grand. Everywhere we looked was beautifully detailed architecture. The ceilings were ten feet high with large crown moldings, and there were multiple oak colonnades on the entry to the living room. The stairway was solid oak trimmed with oak paneling. At the second landing, there was a six-foot stained glass window. To our left was a large living area also paneled in oak, and it housed a huge fireplace on the south wall. On our right was a large formal cherrywood–paneled dining room, with a curved fifteen-foot window bench and bay windows made with curved glass.

Just off the living room to the west was a formal library paneled in cherrywood. Between all the rooms were solid cherry or oak pocket doors. In between the kitchen and the dining room was a walk-through pantry that created floor-to-ceiling storage made of oak with a built-in counter. The kitchen opened up to a big room with a huge central island for preparing meals. To the west, there was a rear exit that led into the back porch and out to the backyard.

Next, we made our way upstairs to the second and third floors. They were not as ornately trimmed, but the rooms were still spacious. The second floor was used as a dormitory room for housing up to fifteen girls. There were also two other small rooms where live-in counselors would stay while working in the ministry. After the second floor tour, we climbed to the third floor. This whole floor was to be our apartment. It had a kitchen, bathroom, two bedrooms, and a living area. A basement of equal size was used for storage, classrooms, and offices for the ministry. When this house was built, no expense had been spared. The house was previously owned by the Creighton family. It was their summer house in the country. (The house is located just off of NW Radial Highway in Benson Township.) After our tour, we spent the rest of the day meeting all of the students and the ministry staff.

Pam and I knew the Lord had led us here, and we were anticipating the good things he was going to do in us and the ministry. We got settled in, and Pam's parents brought all our wedding gifts that we had not had with us in college. We had more space in this house apartment, and Pam was excited to make our house a home by using our wedding gifts. On our first day of work, Larry and Sue took us to the main office and introduced us to the office staff and Roger Helle, the director of the ministry. Roger was a funny man who was a Vietnam veteran. His stories were wonderfully intriguing. He had many scars and stories of God's dealing in his life through his marine career. His job was to keep the ministry going by raising support, so he spent much of his time on the road talking about Teen Challenge and what God was doing in him and the ministry. Pam and I spent the next couple of weeks working during the day shift with Larry and Sue to learn the ropes of the ministry and the history of all the girls staying at the house. This began another life-changing roller coaster ride no one could have anticipated.

PRAYER CHANGES THINGS

THOSE FIRST FEW weeks went by quickly. Each counselor who worked for the ministry was assigned a few girls and was responsible for their learning and development. We were given responsibility over a student named Sandy who was battling depression and suicidal thoughts. Pam and I listened as she told her life story, trying to get to know her better and discover the root of her issues.

At the same time, I felt stirred to begin praying and fasting for the ministry and the condition of the house. Ever since we arrived at Teen Challenge, I felt distraught over the presentation of the house and how that reflected on the ministry. I felt as if God wanted to change the image of the house to bring it up to a new level. I took down the aged Teen Challenge sign because I felt so strongly it needed to be improved.

At the next staff meeting, Roger asked if anyone knew where the sign was because he had noticed it was gone. I couldn't bring myself to admit I had taken it down and hidden it. Fortunately, he didn't press the issue and didn't seem that concerned. The next week I began fasting and praying. I lay on my living room floor with my Bible open, praying and asking God to change the house and ministry for the better. While beating the floor with my fist, I kept pleading with him over and over to hear me and to answer my prayer because I knew that he wanted to change things. This went on for four days. Once I felt a release from my fast, I left the issue in God's hand. I knew the Lord heard me, and I knew he would answer. I didn't know when, where, or how; but I knew he heard me, and I trusted him to bring the change about.

Needless to say, things started happening. Usually when a person begins to pray and take hold of heaven, things start to happen, but not everything is good or the way he expects it to turn out. When believers pray, they make the devil mad, and he fights back and tries to destroy or discourage them from doing good or continuing to pray. And so it began with the fire alarm system in the house. It started going off for no apparent reason. We were also having some unusual problems that were arising out of nowhere with the girls. For several weeks, the fire alarm system was acting up, so we unplugged it until we could afford to have someone come and evaluate the problem.

One night, we were awakened by the sound of the fire alarm once again. I had unplugged it before we went to bed, but it started going off. The alarm system had a battery backup that made it work, so unplugging it didn't always help the problem. That night I went downstairs to investigate what had set off the detector. I checked out the second floor, the first, and then the basement. I hated going into the basement at night, but I made my way down there and discovered the detector by the basement entry door was tripped. It seemed strange this was happening often and for no apparent reason. It was becoming a joke around the house. We were no longer surprised when the fire alarm went off, and nobody got excited thinking there was a fire. It completely dulled our senses to the idea that there could be an actual fire.

URGENCY!

EACH MONTH, THE house employees received a four-day weekend because during the week we had only one day off. Pam and I had been there for a few months, and our four-day break was coming up. I was looking forward to the time off and being able to go to Pam's folks'. It had been a stressful few months with learning about the students and coping with all the unusual activity concerning the fire alarms. Pam was expecting our first child, so the thought of becoming parents was also weighing on me.

The day before Pam and I were supposed to leave for a break, I kept feeling like I needed to get out of town. It felt as if someone were going to drop a bomb on Omaha, and I wanted to get out of town before it happened. I kept telling Pam I felt a storm on the inside compelling me to take off running and not stop. I didn't know why I felt this way, but it was overwhelming. It was unusual for me; it felt very urgent. I told Pam that as soon as our shift was done at 11 p.m., we were leaving town.

Because we were going to have a baby, I had decided to buy a bigger car. The car we had was a little two-door Chevy Chevette, and it was much too small to get a baby (and all the necessities) in and out. Pam and I had saved a small amount of money, so we bought a brand new 1984 Chevy Cavalier. This was the first brand-new car I had ever owned. We loaded up the new car and made our way north out of town. As I was driving, I kept feeling that same urgency, so I kept praying in the spirit. Sometimes when we do not have words, the Holy Spirit will commune for us. Romans 8:26-28 says:

> In the same way, the Spirit helps us in our weakness. We do not know what we ought to pray for, but the Spirit himself intercedes for us with groans that words cannot express. And he who searches our hearts knows the mind of the Spirit, because the Spirit intercedes for God's people in accordance with the will of God.

When we use our spiritual gift of tongues in our prayer times, God's Spirit intercedes on our behalf and speaks mysteries to God through intercession that brings us edification. In other words, God helps us to pray even when we don't know what to say. His Spirit will give us the words to speak that will bring us help in our time of need. In 1 Corinthians 14, this gift of the Holy Spirit is explained. It would benefit Christians greatly to know how to receive and use their God-given, heavenly language in prayer. The warfare we wage is unseen, so God sends us help through our prayer language to encourage us and speak against those unseen demonic powers.
2 Corinthians 10:4–5 says:

> For the weapons of our warfare are not carnal, but mighty through God to the pulling down of strongholds, casting down imaginations, and every high thing that exalts itself against the knowledge of God, and brings into captivity every thought to the obedience of Christ.

DEER IN THE HEADLIGHTS

W E WERE ABOUT five miles past the town of Fonda, Iowa, when all of a sudden to my right appeared a deer's head illuminated by my headlights. The doe was coming up out of the ditch. I swerved to the left to try to miss the deer. Pam was asleep in the front passenger seat, and as I swerved the car to my left, the deer's head crashed into the windshield on her side. The deer's body hit the front right fender and both doors on the passenger side. Pam screamed. The deer went flying and ended up on the side of the road.

I looked over at Pam and asked her if she were okay. She said she was a little startled but fine. I looked out my window up toward the starlit sky and told God, "It doesn't matter what happens to me. I still believe in you." I was thankful neither of us was hurt, and I thanked him even though I was distraught because my brand-new car was just demolished by a hapless deer. We arrived at Pam's folks' around 2 a.m. safe and sound.

FIRE!

THE NIGHT WAS restless. In the morning, Pam and I got up and ate breakfast and told her parents about the deer accident. While we were still talking, the phone rang. Pam's mother answered the phone, and the person on the line asked for me. I took the phone, and it was Roger. His voice broke. "Chuck, Sandy committed suicide last night. It started the house on fire. No one else was hurt, but some of your things were destroyed. So when you come back from your break, we will have to talk about living arrangements and what we're going to do from here."

I hung up the phone in disbelief. We all sat there in shock, trying to absorb everything. Pam began crying. I felt numb. Pam and I did not hurry back to Omaha; we stayed at her folks' house preparing ourselves emotionally for the return. When it was time to go back, Pam's parents decided to go with us and help with the cleanup. I appreciated the support because we needed it.

Filled with hesitation, we started the three-hour trip back. We knew what lay ahead might be harder to swallow than we were willing to admit. When we arrived at the big, white house, we hardly recognized it. The windows were broken and trash covered the front yard. The entire north side of the house was scorched. Larry and Sue greeted us with hugs and tears. They felt bad that we had just moved in, and all our things were heavily smoke-damaged or destroyed.

Walking through the house, we were overcome by the piercing stench of smoke and the sight of the damage. The house was a mess. Larry said all our things had been moved out of the house and into a warehouse for storage and protection. When we walked up to the third floor, there was nothing but empty rooms with smoke, water, and fire damage. The fire had run up the pipe chase to the second and third floors from the kitchen area. As Larry and I were walking throughout the house, we felt a demonic oppressiveness in the air. Everyone involved with the ministry did not sleep for about three nights. The attacks of the enemy were strong, and everyone reported feeling the same thing. The event of Sandy's death was tragic, but I also knew that "In all things God works for the good of those who love him, who have been called according to his purpose" (Romans 8:28).

After Larry, Sue, Pam, and I had taken a tour of the house and seen its destruction, we went to Larry and Sue's home. Larry said it was about 6:00 in the morning when the fire alarms started going off. One of the live-in counselors got out of bed and casually walked to the door at the top of the stairway thinking it was just another false alarm. When she opened the door, smoke started rolling through the opening into the second floor. She started screaming, "Fire!" but no one believed her at first.

Then they saw the smoke, and they all started scrambling to get everyone out. The counselor called the fire department from the next door neighbor's phone, and they arrived a few minutes later. The kitchen and pantry area were already engulfed in flames.

They began to break windows around the kitchen and pantry area. After a few minutes of work, they had the major flames knocked down and were working on breaking through the wall to kill the flames going up the pipe chase to the second and third floors. When they had gotten the flames completely knocked down in the kitchen, they found Sandy's body.

GOD'S PROVISION

THE FIRE BROUGHT a lot of attention to the ministry of Teen Challenge. The local TV stations and newspapers did interviews and articles about the tragic event. With all of the media coverage, people started calling and offering their help with the cleanup and finances.

In spite of the tragedy, Sandy's family was not bitter. Instead they were very thankful for the ministry of Teen Challenge. They knew it made a difference in Sandy's life because she told her family she was the happiest while she was there. Even though this was such a tragic event, we began to see God's hand even in the worst of situations.

Over time people started discovering more about Teen Challenge and what our purpose was. We started getting phone calls from businesses, local retailers, and contractors saying they wanted to donate items and labor for the rebuilding of the house. One building contractor called and donated all the siding for the reconstruction. We had a local retailer call and say they wanted to donate all the new carpet and flooring. Others called to donate food, clothes, dishes, and other building materials such as windows, countertops, and labor.

Jesus was taking care of all our needs. The house was being rebuilt, and Jesus was answering my prayers; although I must admit, I didn't think it would happen in this way. How often do we pray for things and expect them to happen one way, but the answer comes about in a way we did not expect. Sometimes Jesus allows hardship and suffering, so we may walk into the blessing of the Lord. Sometimes a blessing of the Lord starts through pain and grief but ends up bringing us to a new maturity level and stronger faith.

LARRY AND CHUCK
IN A TRUCK

AFTER ABOUT A year, the house was completely restored. Larry and I both worked with the contractor to rebuild the house and make the improvements that were needed for the use of the ministry. A short time later, I retrieved the sign I had hidden, and we repainted it and hung it back up. Larry and I spent a lot of time moving furniture from warehouse to warehouse. We joked about starting a moving business called Larry and Chuck—Two Men and a Truck. "If you got it, we can move it" would be our motto. We had a lot of fun together and would crack jokes all day long. One day we received a call from a woman on the other side of town who wanted to donate a couch, so Larry and I headed out to her house to pick up the couch, hoping it was one that the ministry could use.

Once we arrived in the area where she lived, we noticed how well-kept the neighborhood was. This seemed a good indicator that the couch would be in good condition. We arrived at her house, walked up to the door, and rang the doorbell. The woman came to the door and said, "Oh yes, the couch is in the garage. I will go open the big door. You guys can meet me in the garage." We walked over to the garage as the overhead door was opening. We looked over the edge of the car and were shocked. The couch was old, sagging, and covered with holes and cat hair. As we walked toward the couch, we could smell urine on the material.

Larry and I looked at each other in disbelief. This lady called us to donate a couch that was only worthy of the dump. We couldn't believe she wanted a full tax write-off for this junk. It proved to us that looks are deceiving and things are not always as they appear. Larry and I loaded up the couch and hauled it to the dump.

Later that week, someone called and said he wanted to donate a van to the ministry. Larry and I were excited about this, and we went to pick up the van. When we arrived at the address, we saw the van sitting out front. As I walked up, I could see light from one side to the other through a rust hole. Larry got the title and the keys from the owner, and the owner said he wanted a full tax write-off. I was shocked by what I heard. Larry obliged, and then he threw me the keys and said, "I'll follow you home." I got in the van and tried to start it. After about a minute of cranking, it finally started, and I put it into drive and started moving around the cul-de-sac out to the first stop sign. I didn't notice that the brakes didn't work until after five or six pumps. I rolled out into the intersection and was relieved that there was no traffic coming.

It was one scary ride on the way home. It felt like I was on a decrepit roller coaster; everything on that van needed to be replaced. I was drenched in cold sweat, so nervous that someone would stop me or I wouldn't be able to stop myself. By the grace of God, we made it home. I felt lucky to be alive. We were able to get a junkyard to come and pick up the van… thank God.

This is my recommendation: Do not give anyone anything you wouldn't want yourself. If it's a burden to you, it most likely will be a burden to someone else. Instead of giving away our burdens, we should learn to give away blessings. When we bless someone, it usually costs us something that we consider valuable whether it be money, time, or things. I'm reminded of the Scripture verse that says, "Be not deceived, God is not mocked. For whatsoever a man sows, so that shall he also reap" (Galatians 6:7). If you give junk, you're going to get junk in return. But if you bless someone with something that costs you, then you'll reap an eternal reward; and someone may bless you with something better than what you gave away.

After a few more months of moving furniture and helping with construction, the house was completely rebuilt and it looked brand-new. We felt we should dedicate this house officially to the Lord for his purposes. We gathered all the staff and students in front of the house. Roger said a few words, and then we prayed and gave thanks to God for what he had done in giving us this huge blessing.

Pam and I learned many things about ministry while working at Teen Challenge, but I believe the main thing I learned was how to deal with spiritual warfare and different personalities. Just as the Holy Spirit is seated in our hearts in love, the devil works in the hearts of people through their seeds of resentment. If we let these seeds of resentment persist in us, this will give the devil a foothold. That's why it's vitally important that we learn to forgive and receive God's healing, so the enemy can't have what he needs to work. Jesus said to forgive and you would be forgiven (Matthew 6:14). He gave us the laws of the Spirit for our protection. For example, when a child reaches for a hot pan on a stove and we say to him or her, "Don't touch that. You'll get burned," we are looking out for the safety of the child. The same thing is true for the laws of the Spirit. They are there for our protection so we don't get burned.

I have learned that Jesus' commands are not to kill our joy but to protect us from hurting ourselves. He sees the whole picture, and we only see in part. Trust him who sees from the start to the end. He is a good God who gets blamed for too much of the devil's work. The Bible teaches us in 1 Peter 5:8 that the devil is like a roaring lion looking for someone to devour. Jesus always has his people's best interests in mind; the opposite is true of the enemy. I say trust God, get to know his Word, and then you won't be taking swings in the dark hoping you land a good punch. John 8:32 says, "Then you will know the truth, and the truth will set you free." The truth I am speaking of is the Word of God, nothing else. Everything else is half-truths coated with distractions.

THE FRONT LINES

D ISTRACTIONS COME IN many different forms. New students, one of which was involved in witchcraft prior to coming to us, arrived at Teen Challenge. Needless to say, this student had suffered a very abusive past, which caused her to be filled with resentment. She injected all sorts of distractions especially during prayer times with the group. When we were in a prayer circle, I regularly whispered the name of Jesus in worship. She stood right next to me saying under her breath, "Stop saying that," because it caused her to become very agitated. It opened my eyes to the fact this was probably a demon spirit. Larry noticed her problems earlier and agreed with me that she probably had a spirit that needed to be dealt with. So we took some of the staff to one of the offices to pray in agreement and ask God for wisdom on how to pray. We did this because there was no set formula for the work of the Holy Spirit, especially regarding deliverance. In this person, deliverance had not yet come because of her unwillingness to forgive. Also if the person you are praying for does not want to be delivered, then she probably will not. There has to be a willingness and desire from the person you're praying for in order for him to receive deliverance. Whether or not a person believes this, the fact is there are all kinds of spiritual activities going on all around us. We live our lives on the front lines every day.

2 Corinthians 10:3-5 says:

> For though we live in the world, we do not wage war as the world does. The weapons we fight with are not the weapons of the world. On the contrary, they have divine power to demolish strongholds. We demolish arguments and every pretension that sets itself up against the knowledge of God, and we take captive every thought to make it obedient to Christ.

We also saw people who were set free from demonic oppression, and their whole countenance changed. We could literally see the lights come on behind their eyes. It was an encouraging manifestation of God's power working in them. When I was first introduced to deliverance ministry, it scared me because I didn't know much about it except through my reading of the Bible. To read about it and to actually do it were two different things. Teen Challenge forced me to grow up.

GOOD NEWS, BAD NEWS

W E HAD BEEN at Teen Challenge for one year and had learned many things. Pam had come to full term, and we were looking forward to the delivery of our first baby. The due date was the last week of December, but it was now January, and the baby was two weeks late. So our doctor scheduled an early morning labor induction. After fourteen hours of labor, an exhausted Pam delivered Josiah. We both were thanking God for our healthy firstborn son. I began making phone calls to all our relatives to announce the good news. I called my parents and my brothers. The last phone call I made was to my grandparents, telling them the good news. Then they asked me if I had heard anything yet, and I said, "What do you mean?"

Then Grandma said, "Your dad has leukemia." I stood there in shock. I didn't know what else to say. Grandma was distraught, and I could barely breathe.

When I hung up the phone, Pam was still lying on the bed with little Josiah. I turned. "Dad has leukemia." I plopped in the chair. I couldn't believe I had just become a father, and that same day I found out my dad had leukemia. It was getting late, and I was thinking about going home and sleeping in my own bed. I couldn't bear the thought of sleeping at the hospital. I told Pam I was going home to try to get some rest. We enjoyed our son together for a time. Then I said my goodbyes and went out to my car.

It was January in Nebraska, and we were having a cold snap. I got to my car, opened the door, sat down in the driver's seat, and began to crank the engine. It wouldn't start. I attempted a few more times to get it started with no luck. So I traipsed back up to the room, and when I walked in, Pam was surprised to see me. The nurse overheard my tale of woe and said I could stay in Pam's room on a rollaway bed for the night. By this time, I was exhausted and accepted her offer. Our new little family spent its first night together in a hospital room in Omaha, Nebraska.

The next morning, I called Larry, and he came to the hospital with jumper cables. He was happy to hear the good news about Josiah and sorry to hear the news about my dad. Larry is a man full of faith. He suggested we pray and agree that God would be glorified through all this. I was thankful for a friend like Larry. The car finally started, and I arrived home. I walked into our apartment bathroom and began filling up the bathtub with hot water. I couldn't wait to sit in that hot water and release some of the tension I had accumulated over the last couple of days. Once I stepped into the tub, the warmth of the water engulfed me. Sliding down I just began to cry. The warm water felt so good, and I could feel the arms of Jesus around me as I began to relax. He told me, "Your father is in my hands. I will take care of him. Now this is what I want you to do. I want you to love your son, like I have loved you. Then you tell him about me."

I began to weep even harder. I have never forgotten what he told me that day. Jesus emotionally stamped me that day while I was sitting in the bathtub. So from that time on, my babies were the focus of my attention, and I cherish each and every moment with them. My family is the most important thing to me on this earth. I love Jesus for showing this to me at a young age. It is easy to get lost chasing after promotions and money, but because of that moment in the bathtub, I have wholeheartedly made my family a priority. Jesus said in Matthew 6:33, "But seek first His kingdom and His righteousness, and all these things will be given to you as well."

TELEVISION IN IOWA

A S JOSIAH STARTED growing and demanding more of our time, it was taking away from our effectiveness in the ministry at Teen Challenge. It was time to move on, so I found a job in Fort Dodge working as a mechanic, which moved us from Nebraska to Iowa. Pam and I found an old farmhouse south of town to rent from some family friends. The first few years there were difficult. Finances were tough, but we continued to plod on. After working as a mechanic for six months, I tried selling insurance. Times were difficult, and people weren't eager to spend money on insurance, so after a short stint, I was unemployed. Being a man without a job can be ego crushing. During this time of unemployment, I did odd jobs to make money, but it was difficult; and all I could do was cry out to God for help. In this time of desperation, I took my Bible and went behind the machine shed and asked Jesus if we were to stay in Fort Dodge or move somewhere else and find work. He spoke these words to me found in Jeremiah 29:5-7:

> Build houses and settle down; plant gardens and eat what they produce. Marry and have sons and daughters; find wives for your sons and give your daughters in marriage, so that they too may have sons and daughters. Increase in number there; do not decrease. Also, seek the peace and prosperity of the city to which I have carried you into exile. Pray to the Lord for it, because if it prospers, you too will prosper.

After reading this, I was encouraged to stay in Fort Dodge and continue to plod on.

The bills were beginning to pile up, and I didn't have enough money to pay them. We needed about $500. I told the Lord, "If you called me here, help me to stay here and provide for our needs."

Later that week, I picked up the mail, and we had received a $500 check. The sender was someone we knew but who was oblivious of our current situation. God was aware of our situation, and we were so thankful for his provision. Jesus is awesome! A few months later, I found a job at Iowa Central Community College working in the college media center. I felt at home with this job and enjoyed it very much. I liked the college environment and being around younger people. While working in the media center, the college started a new interactive instructional television system that could reach a nine-county area. They hired a young man named Mark to work on the technical development and maintenance of the network. They gave Mark an office just down the hall from mine. Mark and I developed a good friendship. We had a lot in common, so it was easy to talk with him. As I got to know Mark and found out more about his life and the hardships he had gone through as a kid, I was surprised he didn't seem bitter. Mark appeared cautious in our conversations about faith and life, but his curiosity rose as he witnessed the peace that was constant in my life. He did a pretty good job of hiding his tumultuous past, but the more we talked, the more I learned to recognize he was in turmoil.

Mark and I would spend a lot of time talking in his office. We started talking about God, and I told him how I became a Christian and how that changed my everyday life. This caused Mark to examine his own thinking. He told me later he was always listening for something he could refute. The problem was he never heard anything he disagreed with. This sparked a curiosity in him. He started to recognize there was something much larger than us at work. The idea that God was trying to get through to him brought him some anticipation because, just maybe, there was something to this faith thing.

After a short time of working in the media center, the vice president asked me to come to his office. When I arrived, he indicated a chair and told me they were offering me a job working with Mark in the interactive television department. This was great news. I was getting a job I hadn't even asked about, working in an area that I thought was fascinating, and getting to work with Mark at the same time. We were already good friends, so the offer was very appealing. My job was to be a control room manager for the network. Mark knew nothing about the job opening and was just as surprised as I was. Looking back, I can see the Lord put us together so we could speak into each other's lives as we matured.

MARK MEETS HIS MAKER

MARK AND I started plugging away at getting the television system on the air. We were learning a lot about broadcast television. At this time, Mark had not yet surrendered to Jesus. I tried not to hammer him too much so he wouldn't feel pummeled by my constant talking about Jesus. I kept praying for the Holy Spirit to do his work in Mark and bring him to salvation through Jesus. One morning when I was setting up the computer program for the next class, Mark came into the control room and put his arms up on the back of the TV monitors and said, "Well, do you notice a difference?"

I said, "What difference?"

After a long pause and a look of surprise on his face, he said, "I asked Jesus to take over my life."

I said, "You did? That's great news!"

"You couldn't see it on my face?" he asked.

"Well, Mark, I didn't look real close at your face. That's wonderful news, dude!" Mark proceeded to tell me that when he was down in the transmitter shack at the base of the tower, he had the door open and was sitting there thinking about his life and all the problems he had. He said, "Lord, if you're for real and you can help me get out of these problems, then make it rain outside." As soon as he was done speaking this short prayer, he looked up and, to his amazement, saw raindrops starting to fall across the horizon. He told me right there he knew Jesus was for real and that he needed him in his life.

I had previously explained to Mark how to receive Jesus, and he said at that moment he bowed his heart and asked Jesus to forgive him of his past and present sins. He said he felt like a burden had dropped off his shoulders and a tight band released from his head. He said the release brought tears to his eyes. I knew something had changed Mark on the inside. I said, "Mark, this is just the beginning. God has much more in store for you."

Mark had made the step of faith, and now he was seeing what was on the other side of his decision to follow Jesus. That is the unique thing about the kingdom of God. While a person is trying to decide whether or not he wants to make that decision to follow Jesus, he may or may not get a snapshot of what the kingdom of God looks like. It is not until one actually humbles himself and takes the step of faith that he can see the full picture of the kingdom of God and the blessing that it is.

Now that Mark was a Christian, our friendship went to a new level. Now we were Christian brothers, so we spent a lot of time talking about Jesus and his return. We spent time praying for the salvation of friends and family and talking about kingdom principles and practical life applications. We also prayed for the college campus and the spiritual life there. He was amazed at how easy some of the answers to life's problems were resolved with prayer and how God did miracle after miracle.

REBEKAH'S TROUBLES

P AM WAS PREGNANT with our second child, Rebekah. A good friend of ours, Dr. Brian Welch, was Pam's obstetrician. We attended the same church. I would usually go with Pam for the checkups, so we could listen to the heartbeat and see how things were developing. During the first few months, everything checked out fine. About halfway through the pregnancy, I noticed Rebekah's little heart would skip a beat here and there. To my surprise, Dr. Brian didn't act shocked or say anything about the skipping heartbeat.

Toward the end of the pregnancy, we were in his office for a weekly checkup, and we were listening to her heart. I still noticed it seemed to be missing beats. This time, Dr. Brian said something. "The last few months I have been noticing that her heart seems to be skipping beats. I don't think it's anything to be concerned about, but I think we should take an ultrasound of her heart just in case there are any issues we can't see. I also want to make an appointment with a specialist just to be on the safe side." Pam and I were a little concerned, but I must admit I felt in my spirit that everything was going to be okay even though we had every reason to be upset. Brian suggested we agree in prayer, so right there in his office, we took one another's hands and began to ask God for wisdom, healing, and a good report from the specialist.

After the ultrasound, the radiologist concluded that he could only see two chambers in Rebekah's heart. Brian gave us his report but offered to take a look himself with another ultrasound. He said he had some time after his office hours and would be happy to take a second look. We called our family, pastor, and friends to pray. Brian began the ultrasound, and we all stared at the monitor. He said, by what he could see, all parts of the heart looked normal. He said, "Just to be safe, we will have a specialist take a look at the images."

A few days later, Brian got the report and requested that we come in to talk. On our way, we couldn't help but feel anxious. We were fearful that the news might not be good, but yet we also felt a peace. He told us that the specialist saw some possible problems with Rebekah's heart rhythm. Brian's recommendation was to go to Des Moines for the delivery, but Pam and I both felt at peace with staying in Fort Dodge to deliver the baby. All we could do at this point was wait and pray. In prayer, we agreed that God would direct us and help with the delivery of Rebekah.

Within a week, Pam started having contractions, and we went to the hospital. Brian was paged and arrived a few minutes after us. Everything was prepared for the delivery. They strapped a heart monitor around Pam's stomach to keep an eye on the heart-beat of the baby. During each contraction, her heartbeats would slow down or stop for a moment. I knew the heartbeat's dropping out like that was not good. Well into labor, the contractions were getting more intense and longer, which was putting more stress on little Rebekah's heart. I could see concern on Brian's face. In between one contraction, Brian asked both of us if we wanted to do a C-section for quick delivery. Both Pam and I contemplated that for the next few minutes, but we both felt at ease about a natural delivery and stuck to the original plan.

I could tell by the duration of the contractions that we were on the homestretch. I kept praying in the spirit, asking God to deliver this baby normally and in good health. And finally, little Rebekah was delivered into the hands of Brian. She had good color, and she screamed out a couple of good cries, another good sign. Brian gave me the honor of cutting the umbilical cord. Then little Rebekah was hurried off to the ICU nursery area.

They took an EKG of Rebekah's heart and found the heart function was normal, and there were four chambers in the heart, not two, like first thought. But the nerve that regulated the heartbeat was not fully developed, and it was causing the irregular rhythm. The specialists in Des Moines assured us that within a month her heart should be beating normally and no medication would be needed. We were happy to hear this great news.

Little Rebekah gave us a few scares along the way. I must admit, because of the things I was going through with my dad having leukemia, it was stressful to look at little Rebekah with all those monitors and tubes hooked up to her. I was so thankful for the good report. Jesus had healed Rebekah's heart, and we were thanking God for the miracle.

DISCIPLINE OF PRAYER

I HAD TAKEN off a few weeks from work to help Pam at home until she was fully recovered from having a baby. It felt good to get back to work. I really enjoyed my job, and one of the things I enjoyed most was when my presence was needed to assist the professors with technical difficulties and any other problems that might arise. Everything was well maintained, so we didn't have many issues, which I was thankful for. Because of the good maintenance, I would get some free time to pray while working in the control room. When I prayed, I had to get up and move around, or I had a tendency to get drowsy. I would pace back and forth, walking about ten or fifteen steps in one direction, and then turn around and walk the other way. This would keep me alert and focused while praying.

I had many enjoyable times with the Lord in the control room. People would come in while I was praying or just as I finished, and they would mention to me how it felt so peaceful in the control room. I spent many hours praying for the city, the college, and the church. I prayed God would change the whole atmosphere of the city and rebuild the city square. I also prayed he would bless the college and cause it to grow, and that he would send people here to make that happen. I prayed God would cause people to turn toward him and that the churches would become fruitful and effective. One of the things I prayed for was the birth of a Christian radio station in our area. It was something I felt strongly about. Every time I prayed, I kept hammering the throne room of God with these requests.

Sometimes things happen so slowly that when there is change, we may not recognize the differences initially as answers to prayers from years before. Looking back over the last twenty years, I can honestly say things have changed, and all the requests I laid before God are still being answered today. Prayers do not expire. Some prayers outlive the one who prayed. Just because we cannot see an immediate answer does not mean God is not working. I have seen so many times where God has quickly answered specific requests. Others I have yet to see, but one thing I do know for sure: my God answers prayer!

I know we have not arrived; on the contrary, there will always be things that need to be accomplished for the kingdom of God and its administration. A lot of the requests that I listed have been answered: the college has grown immensely and been redesigned, the city square has been rebuilt, and the city has taken on a new form of government that has made many new changes in city development. Thank God for his amazing grace that gives us things we do not deserve. He hears our prayers even in our insufficiencies.

CHRISTIAN RADIO

WHEN I HEARD there was a new Christian radio station being established in Eagle Grove, I had to go check it out. My prayer was being answered! Upon arriving there, I was greeted by Mike, the station manager. He gladly invited me in, gave me a tour of the new facilities, and told me they were going to be on the air within a week. I told him how excited I was to see God answering prayer for this area. After the tour, Mike asked me if I knew anybody that would want to be a weekend DJ. I told him I didn't know of anyone, but I would let him know if I thought of someone. He said he was willing to train whoever was hired, and the person didn't need much experience. That statement got me thinking about doing the job myself.

After some more conversation with Mike, I asked him if he would consider me for the job. He said, "Do you have any experience with broadcasting?"

I said, "Yes, I'm in broadcasting now, but I don't have any on-air experience."

He replied, "That's okay. We can deal with that." To my amazement, once again, Jesus actually let me touch something I was praying for. I was so excited. When I got home, I told Pam everything that had happened that day. I always had a desire to be on the radio, and this dream was now being fulfilled. Within the next few days, I started my training for on-air broadcasting.

It was sign-on day. The radio station had a big open house planned and had invited everyone involved with the new Christian radio station to come and help kick off the first on-air experience. This was the first time there was ever a Christian radio station in the Fort Dodge area, and everyone was excited. The air was charged with anticipation for this new ministry to begin. After the introductions of the KJYL staff, the DJ and I headed back to the studios.

The station manager requested that we play the *Hallelujah Chorus* of Handel's *Messiah* for the very first musical arrangement to be broadcast on KJYL. With everybody's watches synchronized and the transmitter on, we started the CD player. For the first time, KJYL's call letters were heard over the air, and then the music from Handel's *Messiah* began playing. The air was charged with electricity; everyone started to clap, shout, and thank Jesus for the new beginning. It was a wonderful day. I worked every weekend for one year at the radio station and enjoyed it very much.

I saw how important the clock is in broadcasting. A DJ cannot be late because people will notice. I was able to learn the process of recording, playing back tapes, reading the news, and using satellite broadcasts. For me, it was a wonderful experience, and I can still remember all those weekends playing back the Top 20 Countdown on Saturday nights. It was cool to have this experience; I have always been fascinated with technology, and I was thankful for the time I had working for KJYL.

JOSEPH VISION RENEWED

DURING ONE OF my nights of prayer, I heard these words loud and clear: "I want you to pray for yourself tonight." Was that right? I spent my days praying for the city, the college, and many things the Lord laid on my heart, but today was different.

Praying for myself felt selfish, so I tried to ignore that inner prompting. But, as minutes wore on, I felt more compelled to pray for myself. So I began asking Jesus to reveal his plan and purpose for my life and to show me what he wanted me to see. As I kept praying and asking God to reveal these things, I started to get an overwhelming sense that Jesus wanted to prosper me so I could be a blessing to others with everything he was giving me to do. Then the nudge of the Holy Spirit reminded me that when I first moved to Fort Dodge, I was led to read the story of Joseph from the book of Genesis. I saw how my life resembled his life and how much I would have to suffer before the promotion of God would come about.

As the evening went on, his words were reactivated in me, and I began to feel the emotional time-stamp of God once again. Jesus kept repeating it over and over in my mind and encouraging me that he was going to make this Joseph-type anointing happen. In this moment, a sense of unworthiness fell on me. Could I really believe that he wanted to do these things in me? I felt so completely worthless, and this Joseph thing seemed like such a big deal to me, much bigger than what I felt could happen. If this was the Lord speaking to me about such a dramatic unfolding in my life, I would want confirmation from him because this seemed so out there. A dream like this could really be based in selfishness, and I didn't want that to happen. I was excited about what I thought I was hearing, so I started asking him to bring confirmation of the "Joseph anointing." I felt as if the Lord was telling me to speak to my pastor and my wife as my step in faith, and he would move because of the faith shown through my talking with them before the confirmation came.

Later that night, after I got off work, I sat down with Pam and described to her what had happened that day in prayer. While I was talking, I could sense she wanted to believe what I was saying but was having a hard time. I told her I was having a hard time with it also, but I was speaking this by faith, trusting God to confirm his word to me even though it seemed like a pipe dream. After I told her the story, I didn't ask for a response. I said, "Let's pray and ask God to confirm his word for us once again." So we prayed in agreement that God would fulfill his word, and he would be glorified in this.

A few days later, I was able to bring up the issue with my pastor as we were traveling in his car going back to the church. I told him I was going to say something to him in faith that was really out there, and I would appreciate if he would hear me out before saying anything. I wanted him to hear it so if the Lord did confirm what he had spoken to me about the "Joseph anointing" on my life, then my pastor would know himself that God had spoken to me before Jesus confirmed it through someone else. I began to repeat to him everything I had told Pam a few days earlier: what the Lord had shown me that night in prayer about how he wanted to bless me, how Jesus had given me a "Joseph anointing," and that he was going to make me prosperous in everything for the advancement of the kingdom of God.

While I was talking, I could sense some unbelief from him. I expected this because if someone else were to tell me the same story, I would have reacted the same way. I knew the pastor was someone who had to know ahead of time so when God did bring confirmation, he would know, along with my wife and me, that God did speak this to me beforehand. This was my step of faith—a step that could change everything.

NUMBERS 1, 2, AND 3

MY PASTOR INFORMED me that the prophet Bill Hammond was coming to Fort Dodge from Florida. This was the first time he had ever been to Iowa for ministry, and he was scheduled to preach in our church. During that same week, Gary Greenwald, pastor of the Eagle's Nest Ministries in California, was scheduled to speak at the Full Gospel Business Men's Convention in Fort Dodge. My pastor also had a friend named Terry Kruse, who worked in the realm of the prophetic, coming down from Minnesota. I was looking forward to the opportunity of hearing three Godly men speak all in one weekend. As the weekend approached, my expectation of what Jesus was going to do grew. I knew my God could do anything, and I wanted to expect the best.

Time seemed to creep as the weekend approached. I kept seeking the Lord, asking that he would confirm his word. In those moments, I was constantly bombarded with the what-ifs. I second-guessed my initial action of telling others about this deep and meaningful word from the Lord. I wondered if I had done the right thing. I doubted that I had heard the words to begin with. I questioned my motives and selfish ambitions. My mind flooded with the criticisms that were sure to run me over when this thing didn't happen.

The weekend finally arrived. I was in high expectation, yet at the same time, I didn't want to be disappointed if no confirmation came. It was Friday night, and Bill was to speak at our church. Anticipation crawled all over me as the service began. Bill, with his southern drawl, testified about his life. He taught about the prophetic ministry, its purpose in the church, and how God was renewing the fivefold ministry in the body of Christ. As he spoke, he often paused as God was showing him something about someone in the crowd. He usually called the man or woman forward, but sometimes he spoke to the person right where he was sitting. Many times there were tears as he ministered prophetically, teaching the Word of God.

I hadn't had much exposure to the prophetic up to this time and had never seen a prophet work in real life. I was smiling from ear to ear watching the Holy Spirit move. It was incredible! Bill was getting to the end of his sermon, and my pastor was standing nearby ready to close the service. Bill started making his way back to the stage but stopped right in front of Pam and me. He looked down and said, "You, with the blue shirt on. God has called you to what I call a Joseph/Daniel ministry. You will have one hand in the business of the world and one hand in the kingdom of God. To draw the two together, you'll take the kingdom of God into the business world, and you will take the business world and the resources and invest them in the kingdom and bring the two together to profit the purpose of God." He continued, "The Lord says he's going to give you a raise and a promotion in the job-related area you are in. It's overdue, it's overtime, and the enemy has tried to block it. God says you prayed and got a little frustrated, but he says he's going to do it for you. Now it is going to come through. It's going to happen. God is going to challenge you to start your own, establish your own, and do your own. You will be the president and head of your own business and your own ministry. Normally, God does not tell people that much ahead of time. He wants you to learn, grow, mature, trust, and be a sower and a giver because God is going to give a lot back to you, and he wants you to be a giver of the kingdom. The devil tried to talk you out of giving because of pressure and problems, but the Lord says, 'I'm going to carry you financially. You won't owe on your house or your car. You won't owe one thing when I get through. You'll make more in one week than you make in a month right now, and you'll make more in a day than you make in a month right now. There will be days I will bring in thousands, and I will prosper you because I have ordained it. All you have to do is walk with me, grow in me, mature in me, and keep both hands fully clenched to that which I have given you, and I will prosper the work of your hands.'"

When Bill Hammond started giving this prophecy, my pastor was standing right behind him. I could see his eyes start to well up with tears as the Lord was beginning to bring confirmation of his work in me. I was amazed at what God was doing. Pam and I were so full of joy that the tears began to flow. Jesus showed himself so faithful to us once again. It proved to me how intimately involved God desires to be in all our lives, how he wants to touch each one of us on a very personal level, and how amazing his love is.

Never give up chasing after him because there is always more of him to be revealed in us and in those around us.

That next evening, we arrived at the Full Gospel Business Men's meeting at one of the hotels in town. Gary Greenwald was speaking in the service. I was looking forward to hearing him because

I had seen him before on his television program, and I liked his teaching. There was a large group gathered for the meeting, and we could feel the expectation in the air. The worship was wonderful, and his teaching cut to the heart. There was a sense of anointing as Pastor Greenwald spoke, and he began to prophesy over people during the service. Toward the end of the message, he started making his way through the crowd talking to different people. I was sitting in an aisle seat with my wife next to me, along with my pastor and his wife. The service was basically over, but he was still walking around encouraging people and giving them prophetic words. I was fascinated by the work of the Holy Spirit in ministry to other people, and I was taking it all in.

Gary was ministering to some people close by, and when he finished, he stepped out into the aisle and looked directly at me and held out his hand. I reached out to take his, and he said to me, "Stand up, Joseph," loud enough so everyone around could hear. I stood up, and he continued to prophesy by saying, "Your life is like Joseph's. Evil men assailed you and plotted against you, but God is making their schemes work for your good and blessing. There is a great call on your life now. It may seem as though you are in the desert being stepped on, but God is bringing you through. God is healing years of abuse and false accusation like God did for Joseph. When Pastor Greenwald was through prophesying, my pastor started to laugh in joyous agreement with what the Spirit had just revealed.

The previous confirmation had been good enough for me, but the Holy Spirit wasn't finished yet; and once again he confirmed the Joseph anointing. I thought this was so cool that God was again reaffirming, in the presence of others, the things he had previously spoken to me. I was in awe at the way this was unfolding. I didn't understand why God would do this for me in such a dramatic way. I've come to realize that God wants this for everyone; he wants to speak into our lives because he loves us so much.

The day following the service with Gary Greenwald, we were having a special service at our church with Bill Hammond and Terry Kruse. Pastor Terry had arrived that afternoon. He knew nothing about what had transpired over the past few days.

While Bill Hammond was ministering the Word of God and giving prophecies, Terry turned toward Pam and me and said, "I sense the Lord saying to me that your life is going to be like Joseph's life and that you need to read the book of Genesis and study the life of Joseph. Through that study, you will come to a better understanding of your life."

My pastor was standing close by and heard what Terry was saying to me. We were all shocked; all of us stood there in amazement. Three times God confirmed his word to me in one weekend. I was not expecting this level of confirmation, and I was totally blessed by the abundance of God's goodness to me. Jesus is awesome! I did not deserve anything I received that weekend, and I know it was by his grace that I received this abundant blessing. My heart was full of his joy, and I couldn't wipe the smile from my face. Jesus proved himself to me so directly and with such great strength and manifestation that I knew for sure he was the one and only God.

I am not more special in God's sight than anyone else. I just didn't trust myself and my own emotions after my roller coaster past. I had to learn to trust something bigger than myself, and Jesus was the perfect answer. Because of my shortcomings and failures, I was looking for something bigger than myself to take hold of me. As I have read the Bible, it has convinced me that the understanding of God is unending. I'm not content to be satisfied with where I am in my faith. I desire more and more wisdom, knowledge, understanding, and insight about the things of God. These words of wisdom I have applied in my learning: "No condemnation before examination." We must not let our pride or our limited doctrinal beliefs stand in the way of learning and experiencing the work of the Holy Spirit in our lives. Religious tradition can stand in the way of our learning more about the kingdom as it did with the Pharisees and Saducees in the Gospels. Jesus is big enough to fix us if we screw up. Just keep your eyes on him and don't condemn things before you examine them in the Scripture for yourself. Just because someone you respect (like a pastor or a parent) tells you something, it does not mean it is truth. Search the Scriptures for yourself, and ask God to open up your heart to examine anything you may believe that may not be truth.

I am so glad I was not church-indoctrinated growing up, so when I became a Christian, I was a clean slate. I had no background of preconceived ideas. The devil has a mission to discourage and block the purposes of God from being fulfilled in our lives. We need to recognize it when it happens. It's not that God stops loving us; or if we don't feel his love, it doesn't mean he's not there. His love is eternal and unending. We need to start giving credit where credit is due and believe God for who he says he is and what he wants to do in us. Knowing the Word of God will help us know the difference between what's from the devil and what comes from God. Pleading ignorance will not be an excuse when we stand before Jesus on Judgment Day.

THIRD PACKAGE
FROM HEAVEN

I LOVE THE sound of children's feet running around the house. The Bible teaches that children are a blessing from the Lord, and Psalms 127:4–5 says, "Like arrows in the hands of a warrior are sons born in one's youth. Blessed is the man whose quiver is full of them." I wasn't finished receiving these little blessings from heaven. Pam was pregnant with our third child, Rachel Joy.

During the pregnancy, Pam felt as if the Lord told her this new baby would be a source of great joy, but after Rachel was born, we wondered if we were slightly off the mark. Rachel had long, skinny arms and legs flailing about as she was carried over to the exam table screaming her head off. We got Rachel home from the hospital and the crying continued. It seemed as if it would never stop. At first, we thought we had given her the wrong name, "Joy," but as she grew a few months older, the crying subsided. Rachel did fulfill the meaning of her name and she brings us great joy.

I enjoy my children, and I consider them a huge blessing. I believe that we must invest in them while they're young. One thing I mean by investment is knowing your children so well that when they walk into the room, you can tell whether or not there is something wrong.

This is the barometer I used in my own life. It's not 100 percent foolproof, but it works a lot of the time for me. The way to get to know children is to spend time with them—face-to-face. It's not just going to ball games and school activities, hanging out at the park with them, or going to the shopping mall together—even though those things help. By face-to-face, I mean going to where they are and hanging out with them with no agenda, just being there. What I have found by doing this is that they realize after a few minutes that I'm not there to tell them to do something or to correct them, but I just want to be with them. It shows them I care.

I could spend my time doing many things, and they know that. But, if I'm with them because I want to be with them, they know I care about what's going on in their personal lives. They begin to open up and talk about their friends, what's going on at school, and what's ultimately going on in their lives. The Bible teaches us in Psalms 111:10, "The fear of the Lord is the beginning of wisdom; all who follow his precepts have good understanding." It also says in Proverbs 1:7, "The fear of the Lord is the beginning of knowledge, but fools despise wisdom and discipline."

It is important to know what the Bible says about how we should treat people and how to forgive so the devil doesn't have a foothold in us. We must have a relationship with the Word of God. We have to know what the Word of God says about everyday life. If we've never read the Bible, then we will never be effective and successful in our lives. We may be rich financially, successful by the world's standards, and full of knowledge; but without wisdom, we will be empty inside. We need to understand that true success continues on into eternity. We take success with us after our natural bodies die and we receive our new bodies. In 1 Corinthians 3:10–15, it says:

> By the grace God has given me, I laid a foundation as an expert builder, and someone else is building on it. But each one should be careful how he builds. For no one can lay any foundation other than the one already laid, which is Jesus Christ. If any man builds on this foundation using gold, silver, costly stones, wood, hay or straw, his work will be shown for what it is, because the Day will bring it to light. It will be revealed with fire, and the fire will test the quality of each man's work. If what has been built survives, he will receive his reward. If it is burned up, he will suffer loss; he himself will be saved, but only as one escaping through the flames.

The only thing I can take to heaven with me is my family and friends. This is what real success is.

TOMCAT

W HEN RACHEL WAS born, it had been almost five years since my dad's leukemia was diagnosed. It was a difficult time for all of us. I remember asking God to heal my dad. I fasted and prayed it would happen. My dad had accepted Jesus, and he had changed. We were all thankful for that. Toward the end of his life, we all, especially my mother, spent many hours at Mercy Hospital in Des Moines.

A few weeks before Dad died, I felt in my heart the time was close and he would soon leave this earth. At that time, we had many cats on the acreage where we lived. One of the old tomcats had a broken lower jaw because of an accident. Having the cat put down broke something inside of me, and all my grief was brought to the surface.

Because letting animals go on the farm was commonplace, I was surprised by my strong reaction when this tomcat was put down. But that day I cried for quite some time, kneeling before the Lord pouring out my heart. After being in God's presence.

I felt cleansed and renewed. Jesus had healed me of all my grief through an old tomcat. Jesus knows how to minister to us in our hours of need. He touched me on that day by emotionally time-stamping me once again and carrying me through my hurts. Until the tomcat incident, I thought I had been okay emotionally handling my dad's sickness. It goes to show that sometimes we lie to ourselves to protect our pride and image. We don't see what's really going on inside of ourselves until Jesus gently puts his finger on our hurt.

What Jesus wants is for us to be in right standing, whole, and healed by his spirit of grace, so we can be more effective for his kingdom's purposes. That's why he wants us healed and set free from our past, so we can be effective ministers for him. Denial is a killer. We must be broken before God so he can touch us. Denial will keep us locked in time and unable to move on to the higher purposes of God's work. We must never forget why we are here; we are not here for ourselves but for an eternal purpose. We can see why we were created in Ephesians 2:10, "For we are God's workmanship, created in Christ Jesus to do good works, which God prepared in advance for us to do."

DAD'S PASSING

A FEW WEEKS after the tomcat incident, Dad was feeling worse. Mom took him straight to the hospital in Des Moines. On their way down, Dad mentioned to my mom the hymn *It is Well with My Soul* was going through his head. They got to the hospital at the beginning of the week, and I knew it probably meant another weekend would be spent in Des Moines. In the middle of the week, I got a phone call at work from my dad, and he said he'd just received some platelets and was feeling good; but then he said to me, "I think this is it." I knew what that meant.

I prayed with him over the phone and told him I would be down this weekend. He replied, "I don't think there's much time." I knew in my heart he was probably right. After I finished praying with him, I told him I loved him. Pam and I went to Des Moines on Friday after work. When we arrived at the hospital, we made our way up to the room where Dad was. I met Mom in the hall, and she stopped me and said, "Chuck, your dad looks different, so when you see him, be prepared."

When I entered the room, he was sleeping, and the light above his bed was on. It was dark outside. I walked over to his bedside and tapped his shoulder. He woke up startled and looked up at me. Mom was right; his eyes were pools of bright blue light. It was uncanny; his face looked angelic. I had never seen his face look like this. It was as if he had one foot in heaven. He could only moan, not talk. Since it was late, I urged him to go back to sleep. I just wanted to let him know I was there at the hospital.

The next day, Dad's breathing started to become shallow and more infrequent. My family was gathered around Dad as he took his last breath. We all stood around his bed crying, and we knew it was over. The pain was deep as I watched my father take his final breath. At the same time, we were all so grateful that he would no longer have to suffer. On our drive home, we felt relieved that the worst part was over. We knew Dad was safe in the arms of Jesus.

When it was time for the funeral, we made all the preparations. Everyone in the family made it back to Iowa, and we all enjoyed being together. It was a blessed time. The service was a time of rejoicing. It didn't have the solemn funeral feeling. We knew Dad was in a better place and was enjoying heaven. We were happy for him. It was a good reminder to all of us that life in this body is temporal, and one day our spirits will live for eternity. It gives me something to look forward to.

INDIA

FOUR YEARS AFTER my dad passed, there was a Full Gospel Business Men's Convention scheduled in Fort Dodge. The speaker was Don Tipton, who was in charge of Friend Ships Ministry. He was a fascinating speaker. He had so many cool stories of faith and how he had stepped out to do God's will, and God provided the means for him and the ministry. He talked about how people would leave their jobs and homes to join the ministry, which would go around the world on ships to deliver all kinds of material supplies to countries in need. I was inspired by his stories and faith. Listening to him gave me encouragement that I could possibly do the same thing. I felt like the Holy Spirit was leading me to join his ministry and go around the world.

As he continued to speak, an overwhelming feeling of doing missions work with him came over me. In that moment, I knew the Lord was speaking to me about doing a faith venture and possibly working with Don Tipton's ministry. After the meeting, my heart being stirred, I took some information about the ministry with me. I got on my motorcycle and started for home, thanking God for speaking to me about my future. When I got to the highway, I could sense a strong presence of the Lord with me as I was giving him thanks for speaking to me.

I was heading north on Highway 169 when I heard the voice of the Lord speaking in my thoughts. He said, "You're not going with Don. You are going to India." His voice was very clear to me, and it shocked me. I knew it didn't originate with me because of the way it came across. I was thinking Friend Ships Ministry, and then, out of the blue, I heard *India*. So I knew this was the Lord speaking. I told the Lord whatever he wanted me to do, I would do. When I arrived home, I shared with Pam everything that had happened that evening: how God was speaking to me, and then the Lord saying, "India." I said if this was the Lord leading me, he would prove himself true again, and we should pray and ask him for his guidance.

A couple of weeks passed, and I was at work in the television control room. The phone rang, and it was Pam on the line. She said our friend from college, Ed Harp, had called. Ed had just talked to David Balasingh. (David was the young man we met while at Central Bible College). David wanted Ed and me to go with him to India for three weeks to preach and minister. Pam and I both knew this was the Lord leading me to go to India. This was the opportunity Jesus had told me about.

There was a part of me that was hesitant to go because I knew it would be difficult. I think that's why the Lord had to tell me beforehand. If the Lord hadn't shown me first, I probably would have found a really good excuse not to go. At that time, there was unrest in India. Furthermore, I feared the exposure to disease and parasites. The idea of being away from my three small children was also painful.

All things considered, I knew the Lord was opening the doors for me, and I had to be obedient. Pam was in agreement, so I made the decision to go. We began the preparations. I sent out letters for financial support, and the Lord sent exactly what I needed. It was another confirmation of the Lord's goodness. We scheduled the flight for December 26, leaving out of Minneapolis. We spent Christmas at home with our families, and the next day, Ed and I drove to Minneapolis with our wives. We had beautiful weather for the trip north.

Arriving at the airport, we checked in our bags, got our tickets, and noticed our itinerary included twenty-seven hours of flying. I must admit, I wasn't looking forward to that. It's difficult to sit anywhere for twenty-seven hours, much less on an airplane. We all said our good-byes and got enough hugs and kisses to last for three weeks. Concealing the heartache of separation, Ed and I boarded the plane for LA. Once in LA, we had a three-hour layover waiting for our international flight. After that interval, we were off again for a flight from LA to Madras. We had three stops along the way: one in Taipei, Taiwan, one in Tokyo, Japan, and the last was in Singapore. On our flight, we chased the sun around the earth's rotation, so the flight was mostly dark. All I could really see were the lights of the cities and open water. We had a ten-hour layover in Singapore, so we were able to take a tour of the city.

Singapore Airlines provided a small room so we could sleep during that ten-hour layover. That was our first significant break during the long trip, and we were able to get in about eight hours of good, solid sleep. I thought I would need about fifteen minutes to shower and get dressed, so about a half hour before the flight was scheduled to leave, I started getting myself together. I didn't realize how big the Singapore airport was. Ed and I were running late when we quickly checked out of our room at the airport. We started down the concourse looking for our departure gate. I thought our gate would be close to where our room was. I was familiar with Iowa-sized airports, but this airport was a whole lot bigger. When Ed and I were making our way down the concourse, we heard announcements over the public address system. We heard the last call for our flight, which was leaving for Madras, so we picked up the pace. By this time, we were running at a pretty good rate, working up a sweat. I think the gate attendants saw us running toward them from a distance, and they held the flight.

We arrived at the gate breathing heavily and barely able to talk. We thanked the attendants for waiting for us. They were all smiling, recognizing that we were Americans in a foreign country and out of our element. Ed and I boarded the plane thanking God we didn't miss our flight. Afterward, we found out that Singapore has some of the longest concourses in the world. Next time, I'll know better.

It was a five-hour flight to Madras from Singapore. On our flight, Ed and I struck up a conversation with a young man on his way to India. Ed sat right next to him doing most of the talking. I heard things every now and then but didn't really know what they were talking about. A few minutes into Ed's conversation with the young man, I felt the Lord speaking to me about giving him a word of knowledge. In a break in the conversation, I asked Ed if I could sit in his seat. We exchanged seats, and I introduced myself to the young man and began to tell him what the Holy Spirit was speaking to my heart. I told him, "I felt God was telling me to tell you there is a big event about to happen in your life that is not going to work out like you have planned." I told him, "God said, it will be okay, and don't be discouraged. Jesus will work out all the details." I knew nothing about the young man.

After my speaking with him, he thanked me. I didn't know if he was a Christian, but I felt the strong impression to tell him what I was hearing. After we talked for a few more minutes, I found out he was a successful and popular missionary's kid on his way to India for his wedding. I congratulated him. I felt as if this young man had a lot of prayer support behind him. I believed that Jesus was watching over him because of the prayers of his father. I went back to my original seat, and Ed and the young man continued their conversation. A few days later in India, we ran into this young man and found out what transpired after our conversation on the flight. He began to tell us that his wedding ceremony had been called off due to some unusual circumstances in the family. Even though he was discouraged about the news, he told me the word of knowledge I had shared with him earlier was making more sense. It brought him hope that God was still in control.

Since we were fully rested, the last segment of our flight seemed to go quickly. It wasn't long before we started to see the lights of Madras, India, below. Ed and I were glued to the windows, and we were shaking our heads in disbelief because we were finally in India on the other side of the world. Everything looked different. From above, we could see the streetlights, which were long fluorescent tubes dimly lighting the streets below. There weren't any tall buildings, and the houses looked like ones I imagined would have been seen in Biblical times. All the structures had a touch of Middle Eastern architecture.

Once the plane landed, we started unloading. I couldn't wait to actually see and feel what I thought I would never experience in my lifetime. As we approached the door with our carry-ons, the warmth of the night caressed our faces. We stepped through the door of the aircraft and our nostrils were filled with scents of burning straw, curry, and cow manure. It wasn't a bad smell, just different. We walked into the concourse and immediately knew we were the foreigners. Being 6'2" I could see over the top of most of the people's heads. I stuck out like a sore thumb. The airport was not like anything found in America. Everything was gray and dirty. There were no windows, and everything was open-air. We arrived at the airport around 2:30 a.m., India time. Ed and I made our way toward customs. We were asked a few questions about why we were in the country. Previously I had been told not to mention I was there for ministry but instead to tell them my occupation.

Once through customs, we made our way to the baggage claim. People swarmed everywhere. We stood around waiting. No luck. After a half hour or so, the carousel stopped. We started to get concerned. It was 3:00 a.m. in a country where we couldn't understand the language, and our luggage was nowhere in sight. I began asking God to work out all the details.

Finally, a representative from the airport approached us and said the reason for the delay was that our bags were packed in first, so they were the last to come out. I was grateful to hear our bags had arrived with us. Since our flight was late and the luggage delayed us further, David began to wonder if we had even made it at all. Finally we picked up our bags around 3:30 a.m. and found our way outside to meet David.

David arranged a ride for us to the hotel where we were to sleep for the night. Once we got everything into the car and started our drive to the hotel, the first thing I saw in the road was a bony, scrawny cow, very unlike cows seen in Iowa. She was lying right in the middle of the intersection. I was reminded of a history lesson from elementary school that said cows were sacred in India, and they have the reign of the land. They can go anywhere and do anything they want, even lie in the middle of the road.

When we arrived at the hotel, Ed and I shared a big bed, and David slept on the floor. Ed and I were so excited about being there that we could not sleep. We lay there trying to sleep but just could not. After about an hour or so, I could hear David praying to the Lord with thanksgiving, quietly and earnestly. David took his faith seriously. Being involved in ministry made him a large target of many attacks from the enemy. It was good to have him as a brother in the Lord, and it was a blessing to see such a great example of sole dependency on our Savior.

DRIVING IN INDIA

W E WOKE UP the next day, having had only a couple of hours of sleep, and went back to the airport. David needed to arrange flights to Madurai for our first series of meetings. For some reason, we couldn't get tickets to fly south, so David asked us if we wanted to hire a taxi driver to drive us there. We all agreed it would probably be the quickest way to get there since our flight was unavailable. Madurai has one of the main temples of Hinduism as well as the Assembly of God church pastored by Dudley Thangaiah where we would be holding meetings.

As our trip began, we were mesmerized by all the phenomenal sites. There were people everywhere, even in the countryside. One of the first things I noticed was that highways doubled as sidewalks and social centers—everything is done on and by the road. Driving was a game of chicken. It was a race to win, dodge the cow, cut around the corner, or beat the person about to step into the road to cross. Needless to say, I was terrified. It made me very thankful for traffic laws and road markings that protect us while we are driving in the States.

David mentioned, while we were on our road trip, that on average about six people die on this highway every day. After seeing all the activity on the road, we could understand why, but we also knew that the Lord was with us. Not long after, we saw a dead person on the road. Crying and screaming, people had gathered around the corpse. After seeing that, David mentioned that if someone hit a person on the road and killed him accidentally, the driver must keep driving because if he did stop, the angry witnesses or family members of the deceased would gather around the car and kill the driver. He also said if we were ever in an accident in a rural area, it would take a long time for emergency personnel to get to the accident. Because of that lengthy wait for help, most people would bleed out before help arrived. Just our staying alive in India was by God's grace. A few miles down the road, we saw another dead pedestrian with the same scenario.

During our travels south, we saw a total of six fatalities. People walking on the road simply wouldn't get out of the way. They might move to one side or the other, but they wouldn't turn around to look at what was coming. Literally, they were all accidents waiting to happen.

We had been on the road for around twelve hours, and everyone was getting sleepy, including the driver. It was completely dark, and David and Ed were asleep. David was in the front seat next to the driver, and Ed was next to me in the backseat. I was feeling an urgency in my gut that something bad might happen. I started praying in the spirit, in my prayer language. I was the only one who was fully awake. I woke David up and told him the driver was nodding off, so for the next few miles, David entertained the driver in conversation until we arrived in the next village. We decided to take a break there and let the chauffeur sleep for a couple hours. There are no rest areas in India, so when we had to go to the bathroom, we would tap on the driver's shoulder, and he pulled over. Everyone then walked out into the grassy fields to relieve himself.

After a couple hours of rest, we were back on the road. I didn't realize that Madurai was so far south. Maybe it seemed so far because we had so many delays, and the driving left us on the edge of our seats. The nighttime driving worked a little differently than the daytime. If a driver faced an oncoming car and wanted to beat him through a narrow gap, he would hurry into the passing lane and flash his bright lights at the oncoming car. This would give him the right to pass first. This would often aggravate the oncoming car driver. The drivers would always be in competition to be the first one through the narrow spot or to make a pass. It reminded me of NASCAR, except in NASCAR everyone is going the same direction.

A few hours from Madurai, during one of our stops, David made a phone call to give the church in Madurai an update on our progress. David came back to the car after the call and said he had been talking to his wife. She mentioned that the church felt the necessity to pray and ask for God's protection for us while we were traveling. David said his wife had also felt an alarm in her spirit that we were in possible trouble. This happened about the same time I had told David I felt like we were in a dangerous situation and that the enemy was planning our destruction in a car accident. We needed to pray to destroy the plan of the enemy. I was encouraged by the prayer support we had from the church. After some time had passed, I felt the burden lift, and I knew that everything was going to be okay. We did arrive a few hours late, missing the evening service at Dudley's church, but we were thankful to reach our destination in one piece. We were all very tired, so David checked us into a nice hotel in Madurai. Finally, we were able to settle down for the evening. Pastor Dudley had planned meetings for the next several nights at the church, so we needed the rest to prepare for the times of ministry.

In the morning, I woke up refreshed. I was able to sleep in and get renewed from the long travels. About midmorning, David arrived with four local ministers for a time of prayer. Pastor Dudley was there, and we were formally introduced by David. We sat down in a circle and began in agreement to ask God to bless the ministry times that were before us. While we were praying, Dudley began nodding off in sleep. After the prayer, David explained that Dudley had just arrived from another city where he had been filling in for a pastor who had been martyred. He had been traveling all night on a bus to get back to Madurai.

I was amazed at the difference in the hearts of the leadership in India compared to what I saw in the leadership in the United States. In India, the pastors felt as if every Christian was part of their flock no matter what city they lived in. In America, many pastors tend to their own flocks, not having as much concern for the flocks of other churches. In the United States, there tends to be a spirit of competition between churches that is unfruitful and unproductive. In India, because of the cultural differences and the Hindu religion, believers have to be serious about their Christian faith; they're not allowed to walk the fence.

If one converts to Christianity, his family, more likely than not, will reject him; and he could lose all of his friends. People have to count the cost before they make a decision to follow Christ. There is no material or social advantage to following Jesus in India. A new follower will literally lose everything that he once considered valuable. Most Christians in India have counted the cost and are whole-heartedly committed Christians because their faith changes everything. In the U.S. culture, we try to process God through our brains and have tried to eliminate the need for God in our schools and everyday lives. The problem with merely having a mental assent to God is that it will never create an environment for a good relationship with the Creator of the universe. Jesus needs more than our brains; he wants our hearts. Jesus will never speak through our pride. He is activated in our humility, through a broken and contrite heart. Psalms 51:17 says, "The sacrifices of God are a broken spirit; a broken and contrite heart, O God, you will not despise."

To stay healthy, we made it a practice to eat only in formal restaurants and not eat food from any street vendors—even though the most delicious smells emanated from those street vendor's stands. Most of the food on the streets was cooked over a barrel and handled with bare hands. David said most foreigners get sick if they eat from street vendors. Ed and I were on antibiotics during the whole trip to keep us healthy, and we also had a battery of shots to protect us from various diseases before we made the trip.

Before the evening services, Ed and I went down to the restaurant in the hotel to order things we'd never heard of. Most of the items on the menu were vegetarian meals because of the faith practices in India. When they brought out our orders and we tasted them, we were surprised at how delicious they were. We didn't really miss the meat. The seasoning was out of this world, and everything was perfect. I still miss the way the food tasted.

We also had many home-cooked meals during our stay. The women of the house spent all day preparing food for each meal. They would go out every morning to purchase fresh produce to make these incredibly tasty meals. I still long for a good, home-cooked Indian meal prepared by loving hands. We could tell they put everything they had into preparation, and we were grateful for their heartfelt effort to make us feel at home.

CHURCH IN MADURAI

AFTER AN EVENING meal in the hotel, David arrived to take us to the Assembly of God church in downtown Madurai. I must admit I was experiencing some culture shock. Everything looked as though we had stepped back in time; I was in another world. When we arrived, we walked up to a big open room where people were worshiping God and giving thanks. Then I felt a taste of home. The worship was genuine and powerful. The Spirit of God was heavy in the room, and it was refreshing to again feel the presence of God in worship. It made all the difference in the world to see the congregation gathered together in His name, and it renewed my understanding of why I was there.

We made our way up to the front. Dudley was at the pulpit leading the people in worship. They were singing in the Tamil language. I couldn't understand anything they were saying, but I could feel the spirit of their worship and the presence of God there. I was not on the schedule to preach that night, but they asked if I would pray before the preaching began. I gladly accepted. Their worship, which I really enjoyed, lasted for more than an hour. I believe that worship brings his presence; his presence brings joy; and joy brings strength and peace. There's nothing better than worshiping God.

After the worship was complete, Dudley turned and handed me the microphone. I stood up, and as I took the microphone from him, a strong presence of the Lord fell. I began to pray prophetically that God's anointing was there to restore and heal God's people and destroy the plans of the enemy. I also prayed that the Lord would cause exponential growth in their church and lead many to salvation through the ministry there. The people were in agreement as Dudley translated the words I spoke. The encouraging words of the Lord brought another strong wave of worship over the congregation.

After some time had passed, the worship settled down, and Pastor Ed was called up to preach and minister the Word of God. He had prepared notes for that evening's service and had used them, as is traditionally done in the United States. We were both informed after the service that using notes in India is a sign the speaker is not anointed of God. We were encouraged from that point on to have the sermons in our heads and hearts and not on a piece of paper. Every message from that point on was preached without notes. Jesus certainly was stretching us.

After the preaching, all of us on the platform personally ministered to the people who came forward for prayer. Everyone there used the gifts of the Holy Spirit in ministry; and it was a powerful time with healing, words of knowledge, words of wisdom, and prophecy. Some of the people who came forward were falling down under the power of God, and others were receiving understanding and wisdom as the gifts were being used in faith. It was a great time of God's manifestation and power, and I loved it. The ministry there wasn't a debate over doctrinal issues or theology. It was the ministry of the love of God expressed through his servants. Afterward, we heard of many wonderful testimonies from people of the church who received healing and deliverance by the grace of God.

The service was over around midnight. The beautiful part was no one felt time constraints. They had an understanding that God would give grace to those who did not bow down to time limits. When the Spirit of God was done, they were done. I loved that openness to the movement and work of the Spirit of God. Living in their environment was tough, and church was important in their lives. They were so thankful to be there, and they didn't want to leave. It was refreshing to see people at church because they wanted to be there; they saw it as the most important thing in life. Because of that, they made it a priority, which brought in the blessing of God.

SURPRISE IN A BUSH

T HE NEXT DAY, we were scheduled to minister at a meeting on a coconut tree farm in the country. David said the man who owned the farm was a Christian and wanted his farm to be used for the glory of God. The farm was about an hour or so away from the city. Pastor Dudley had rented a small bus to take a group of ministers and musicians out to our ministry location. It was an enjoyable way to get to know some of the people in his church.

I was able to speak with Pastor Dudley about some of the things the Lord was showing me about the church. On our way, we saw how the farmers worked the fields with a team of oxen that were muzzled to keep them from eating the grain. The Bible teaches us in Deuteronomy 25:4, "Do not muzzle the ox while it is treading out the grain." Because the oxen share in the labor of working the field, they should also share in the harvest. This Scripture teaches we shouldn't be so greedy but be more willing to share with those who labor with us. Here was a live illustration of a Scripture written thousands of years ago.

Once we arrived at the farm, the bus turned onto a lane that led into a huge grove of coconut trees. The palm branches reached out about fifteen feet or so, making them much larger than the trees I recall seeing in Florida or Hawaii. The branches completely shaded the ground underneath. We drove through the grove up to a large, open-sided building with a thatched roof, all shaded by the coconut palms surrounding the building.

I was to have a message prepared for that night and had not yet received anything from the Lord on what the subject of my sermon should be. I was feeling a bit distraught. We arrived early, so we had time to fellowship with some of the people from the congregation and share a cup of coffee with them. But in the back of my mind, I was growing more concerned about what topic the Lord would want me to speak about. Meanwhile, it was pleasant getting to know the pastor of this church and see his heart for the things of the Lord. The coconut farm was beautiful. Each tree was marked with a small, white cross painted on the trunk. I believe this was the farmer's declaration that each tree was dedicated to God. The man who owned the farm was wealthy but understood the true value of wealth. He was gracious in opening up his property for the ministry to the local people. I appreciated his willingness to be a good steward of the things the Lord had given him to manage.

The time for the service was approaching, and I still did not have an idea for a sermon. I kept asking the Lord for the topic of the message. My thoughts were racing, and I was getting nervous. There is always that struggle between the mind and the Spirit of God when a person walks in faith. Because of my nerves, and knowing the meeting could last for quite some time, I needed to use the bathroom before the service. When I walked over to the closest bathroom, I found a line of people waiting. I didn't feel like I had time to wait, so I started to make my way around the back side of the church building.

As I was walking along the side of the building, this thought hit me: *Watch out for snakes.* I knew this wasn't my own idea because it surprised me. I'm an Iowa boy who has only seen non-threatening garter and bull snakes. From that moment on, I was looking down at the ground and beside every bush I walked past. I couldn't hold it any longer, and fortunately I found just the right place to relieve myself. I peered over the bush and detected movement. I looked closely again and saw a huge cobra tail moving into the bush that I was peeing on. It was a good thing I was just finishing, and so without thinking, I turned around and took off running as fast as I could. As I darted through the coconut grove, I was hoping the snake wasn't chasing me.

I didn't care what people thought or how I looked running; I was just praying there wasn't a snake tailing me. If I had been bitten, I probably would not have survived. After running a short distance, I slowed down to take a look behind me and didn't see a snake. I was so glad the Holy Spirit gave me a heads-up concerning the snake in the bush.

Needless to say, I was pumped, and my adrenaline was flowing. With no time to spare, I made my way back to the church building, watching for the snake along the way. When I got inside the church, I walked up to Ed and said, "You're not going to believe what just happened to me a minute ago. I'll have to tell you later." We made our way up to the platform, and I still had not received my message from the Lord. My mind was preoccupied with what had just occurred. Fortunately, when the worship service began, it gave me time to pray and ask God for wisdom for my sermon topic. The worship service went on for approximately an hour, and while I was worshiping, the Lord spoke to me and said I should teach on Jonah chapter 4.

Jonah was sent to Nineveh to preach that the Lord would send judgment in 40 days if they didn't repent of their evil ways.

The people of Nineveh believed the warning and repented. After preaching, Jonah felt sorry for himself because he knew the Lord would forgive them and relent from his judgment. So Jonah went outside the city to wait and see what would happen to Nineveh. While Jonah waited, he built a shelter; and the Lord provided a vine for shade. Jonah was very happy about the vine. But the next day the Lord sent a worm that chewed the vine, and it withered. Jonah was mad when the plant died because it provided him with shade. The Lord had sent the worm to kill the plant to show Jonah that he was grieving over a plant's death and how much more he should have been grieving over the potential loss of the 120,000 souls that lived in Nineveh. Jonah knew the Lord was merciful and would forgive them if they turned to him for help. I spoke to the people about how the Lord longs to forgive us for all our wrongs and heal us of all our sins. I reminded them how much he loves us and wants to show his mercy to us and reveal his truth to our hearts so we may be delivered from our past and be given hope for the future.

When I was finished preaching, Dudley began the altar call by using the gifts of the Holy Spirit to call out people by their first names—people he didn't know—and ask them to come forward to receive from the Holy Spirit the ministry that they needed. This was the first time I experienced calling people out by their first names, using the gifts. How intimate of the Lord to use his servants in such a personal way to show he loves us and calls us by name! It reminded me of the Scripture in John 10:3, "The sheep listen to his voice. He calls his own sheep by name and leads them out."

More people came forward and were moved under the power of God to confess their sins and receive his forgiveness. There were people falling down under the power of God everywhere; nobody could walk in a straight line without tripping over someone. There were people crying and laughing, and all were receiving exactly what they needed from the Lord. All of the ministers were praying for whoever wanted prayer and watching in amazement as the Holy Spirit was being poured out on those in attendance. The people had come from the local village, and some had walked many miles to this meeting. I was impressed by their devotion and how committed they were to receiving from the Lord. Jesus recognized that the only thing these people had was a relationship with him, and he honored their devotion. What a wonderful display of God's power! Thank the Lord that he's all powerful and trumps the devil every time when we are obedient to His word.

When the meeting was over, it was time to go back to Madurai. Everyone involved in the meeting was full of the joy of the Lord, and it was plainly visible on their faces. There's nothing better than having a fruitful time of ministry that brings real joy and fulfillment of purpose to a person's life. Everyone there was experiencing that fulfillment and sensing the joy of the Lord.

I had never preached a message with so little preparation. The message was simple and to the point and definitely directed by the Holy Spirit. I couldn't say pridefully that God had anointed me because of my preparation; I think that's what the Lord was showing me. By his Spirit, and not by the arm of man, all this good was taking place. All the glory goes to him and to his power that works through us when we submit to him. Praise to Jesus. The whole time I was in India, I felt so insufficient and ill-prepared. I knew God had called me to go, but while there, I had the understanding that the trip was more about my learning what Jesus wanted to show me rather than about my ministering to the people. Jesus was teaching me what I needed to know to become more of a man of faith and less of a man of self.

HINDU TEMPLE

WHILE IN MADURAI, during some free time, David took us to the Meenakshi Amman Hindu temple. The temple grounds were so similar to Solomon's temple in the Old Testament that I was amazed. There was an outer courtyard surrounded by walls, and all four walls had a main gate. The gates were towers made up of statues of the different gods and goddesses of the Hindu faith. Statues were built one upon the other to form towers approximately 175 feet high. There were four towers of these statutes, one at each gate. The doorways went right through the middle of each tower. Once within the walls of the temple area, we stood in a huge courtyard surrounding the main temple building where the most holy Hindu gods resided.

Being non-Hindu, we were not allowed into the inner sanctuary. All around the exterior walls of the courtyard were places for lesser gods to reside. Hinduism involves the worship of millions of gods. At one of the gods stationed in the temple, a worshiper could buy a little ball of butter and aim it at the god. If the ball of butter stuck to the statue, it meant the thrower would have a good day. If the butter ball didn't stick, and hit the floor, his day wouldn't turn out well. The floor was littered with butter balls. People who had better throwing arms would do better at sticking the balls. One of the butter balls on the god had stuck right on the middle of the nose. I think that person probably thought he was going to have an excellent day.

The female gods were considered more important in the Hindu religion. The male gods had places of lesser respect. There were people selling all sorts of goods and trinkets within the temple walls and all around the outside of the temple area. People struggle to survive, living day to day in a very spiritually depressed area, serving their many gods, and never knowing anything different. While in Madurai, we could feel the city's spiritual darkness that had been there for many thousands of years. At the same time, when we attended the Assembly of God church just a few blocks away from the temple, we could feel the strong presence of the Lord and the ministry of the Spirit that came through worship and the preaching of the Word of God.

The reason I make a distinction here between light and darkness is because we are in a spiritual war not seen with our physical eyes. The Bible teaches in Ephesians 6:12, "For we wrestle not against flesh and blood, but against principalities, against powers, against the rulers of the darkness of this world, against spiritual wickedness in high places." The whole world is influenced in some way by demonic forces because sin has entered the world. Romans 5:12 says, "Therefore just as sin entered the world through one man [Adam], and death through sin, and in this way death came to all men, because all sinned."

When a person becomes a Christian, Jesus washes away his sins and takes up residence within the person. God's light can shine through us as we surrender to him each day. It is important to note what the Bible says about who Jesus is. In John 14:6 Jesus says, "I am the way and the truth and the life. No one comes to the Father except through me." Acts 4:12 also says, "Salvation is found in no one else, for there is no other name under heaven given to mankind by which we must be saved." These verses make it very clear—the *only* path to heaven is found through a life surrendered to Jesus' work on the cross for our sins. We can't get to heaven through our good works, only through Jesus. In John 10:9, Jesus says, "I am the gate; whoever enters through me will be saved. He will come in and go out, and find pasture." Surrendering my own heart to the love of Jesus and accepting his perfect sacrifice through his death on the cross is the best decision I have ever made in my life.

GOOD OVER EVIL

UDLEY WOULD TELL stories of certain sorcerers who attempted to cast spells and put curses on people to get money. He said if you displeased the sorcerers, they would curse lemons, and then throw the cursed lemons into your yard. Then the demon spirits would attack you with fear, sickness, or death. Dudley said when they started considering him a threat to their money flow and power, they started throwing cursed lemons into his yard. Dudley said when he found a lemon in his yard, he would lift it up toward heaven, and he would thank God for the fresh produce.

The sorcerers were amazed when nothing happened to Dudley or the church members. This was the first time their spells didn't seem to be working, and it made them realize Dudley's God was bigger and more powerful than their gods. This made them afraid of Dudley. For the first time in their lives, the sorcerers weren't rulers over the people, and the demons they served were powerless over Dudley and the Christians there. All this reminds me of the Scripture in the book of Mark chapter 16:15–18, which says:

> He said to them, "Go into all the world and preach the good news to all creation. Whoever believes and is baptized will be saved, but whoever does not believe will be condemned. And these signs will accompany those who believe. In my name they will drive out demons; they will speak in new tongues; they will pick up snakes with their hands; and they will drink deadly poison, and it will not hurt them at all; they will place their hands on sick people and they will get well."

Thank God he has given us authority to tread on the demonic powers of this world and throw down every principality that stands in the way of the kingdom of God. In India, people must serve a God of power and believe in the operation and function of the gifts of the Spirit, or they will be trampled by sorcerers and their demonic powers. In America or Western society, the demonic powers mask themselves because we merely intellectually assent to God, making God and the worship of him controllable and presentable to the human mind and intellect. We think we can fix all our problems with our education and learning. Most of our problems are spiritual and only some are natural. This intellectual assent to God is nothing less than pride, which is idolatry. The idol is man's thinking he can reach God through his mind and not his heart.

SIGHTS AND SOUNDS

AFTER MOST OF the formal ministry was completed, we had a few days to kick back and do some sightseeing before it was time to go back to the States. We were touring along the river near the Krishna Raja Sagara dam area. On the river, people could rent big, round basket boats that held seven to eight people comfortably. The basket boat was huge, and the bottom was covered with tar, making it waterproof. This basket reminded me of a larger version of what was probably used when Moses' mother released him into the Nile River as a baby. It was a unique and exciting experience floating down the river in a real basket.

As our journey began, we enjoyed the views and the bluffs along the river. When we spoke, we could hear the sounds of our voices echo down the canyon. It was definitely a cultural experience. In the basket, there were no seats, so we all had to sit cross legged to make room for everyone in the boat. I was sitting facing outward looking at the scenery and feeling a little uneasy, not because of the basket boat ride but because of some gas pains. I was hoping to keep them undercover and unnoticed and kept trying nonchalantly to let them pass. To my shock, a great thunder came from down under and began a ripple down the canyon walls, scaring the birds out of the trees. I have never been more embarrassed. In a knee-jerk reaction, I looked over at Ed Harp and yelled out, "Ed, come on!" Then in his own defense, he began to deny my accusation. Laughter erupted. What a funny day at my expense. I think it was one of the most hilarious things to have ever happened to me and one of the most embarrassing. My pride was definitely wounded, and I was sorry for being a bit rude. But it didn't seem to upset anyone because later that afternoon some of my fellow travelers told me how my embarrassing incident had brightened their day.

The week of sightseeing in Bangalore, Madras, and Madurai was coming to a close, and it was time to prepare for our trip home. Many other things happened while we were in India, and we learned to love the people and the food. I lost a lot of excess weight eating that wonderfully delicious food. I learned to love curry and all the different seasoned foods the women would spend all day preparing. I still think of the times I spent watching the beautiful sunsets on the roof of David's house, thanking God for the opportunity to be there. Being with the people in that culture, I felt many types of extreme emotion. I also saw that where sin is great, the grace of God was there to raise up the standard higher than the powers of sin. It was wonderful to be there and to live the experience of India and its people. It is something I will always remember.

When I returned from India, I started a new job working for Iowa Public Television. I had been working for Iowa Central Community College in their television department before I left the states. While working there, I completed an electronic radio communications course and then passed the FCC General

Radiotelephone exam. I was then hired as a transmitter engineer for IPTV, set to start my new job upon my arrival back to the states. Something new happened in our home too. That fall (November 1995) little Elizabeth Brianna was born. I had been missing the sound of the pitter patter of little feet running around the house. I was so happy that Jesus had sent us another little present from the throne room. We were now a blessed family of six.

VALLEY OF DESPAIR

ALL THROUGHOUT THIS book, I've expressed how God has brought me many miraculous experiences. But, if I am going to be honest, there is much more to life than the high points and the mountain tops.

Those moments are beautiful and unforgettable, but we wouldn't have them without our valleys. These valleys are different for everyone, and one of my deepest and darkest was depression. I went through a three-year battle with depression, which seemed like the valley of the shadow of death. When I got home from India, I started my new job working for Iowa Public Television. I enjoyed my job very much and was thankful for the opportunity to learn something new.

I had been working a couple of years for IPTV, and after going to college in southern Missouri, I learned to appreciate their mild winters. I forgot how long the winters were and how much darkness came with those long winter nights in Iowa. It was somewhat depressing living through the northern winters again. So, we planned as many vacations to Florida as possible.

On one of our trips to Florida, I decided to send out some résumés. When I went to apply for a job at the UPS warehouse in Naples, Florida, I met one of my brother's friends, John, who owned a public golf course in town. He found out I was looking for a job in the Naples area. We talked for awhile in the parking lot, and I went in and dropped off my application at the UPS warehouse. Back in Iowa after our vacation was over, I received a phone call from John, and he wanted to talk with me about working with him at the golf course as his clubhouse manager. I was thrilled to receive this opportunity to move south and escape the long Iowa winters. So Pam and I made the decision to move to Florida and began to make preparations. I had this feeling in my heart this was not the right move even though everything in my flesh was crying out to leave Iowa and move to Florida.

John and I had hammered out all the details of the job, and I was so excited. But in my spirit, I did not feel the release to move, and this haunted me. I didn't want to tell him, and I fought with it many days. Finally, to my disappointment, I called him and told him I felt like I wasn't supposed to move yet. I felt somewhat relieved, but at the same time I was still warring in myself about the decision. I kept double guessing myself, and my thoughts were racing. I battled with these feelings for some time.

Our life continued to progress, and by the next summer, I called John back and wanted another shot at the job. We made a decision after he put an offer on the table. Once again I struggled with what I was feeling in my spirit, as if this were not the right time. So to my utter disappointment, I sent John a letter and told him how I felt and that I must turn him down again. By this time, I'm sure he was steaming mad and was saying this opportunity would not be offered to me again. I was second-guessing myself on everything and felt very isolated and disappointed about not hearing the voice of God clearly. It was as if I could not hear anything right anymore. In my heart, I felt like a prisoner; I wanted to leave so badly but could not.

While I was in this difficult process of making the decision about whether to stay in Iowa or move to Florida, my friend Ed Plansky came to visit. He was a good friend, and we talked about many things including life issues. He asked me why I wanted to leave Iowa when I had the *Walton* thing going on. In that moment, I realized that God was fulfilling the longing of my heart. When I was a teenager, I used to watch *The Waltons*, longing to have a family like theirs. They were a close-knit family. His question made me realize that even in the midst of the storm, God can reveal his blessing. And even though a person might be focused on the wrong things and be in an emotional whirlwind, he does have the ability to stop and look at the big picture, and realize he has a lot to be grateful for. This conversation opened up my eyes to the fulfillment of a desire that had been within me.

Amazingly, this is not the end of the story. I had two more opportunities set before me to take jobs in Naples, and I declined the first one with no pain. On the second job offer, I was given an opportunity to be a job site foreman for a man my brother knew. Before I looked into this opportunity, I spent some time fasting and praying. Yet, I found myself struggling in my faith and in hearing the voice of God. I was perplexed. After I broke the fast, I started feeling weird in my body. I knew I wasn't myself.

As I started having different symptoms, my mind began to race, and all these voices flooded into my head. The voices were saying things like "You're sick" or "You're going to die." This was when depression set in. I told Pam I felt terrible. My heart was racing, I had pains everywhere in my body, and my skin was turning yellow. After I broke my fast, a burning sensation settled in my feet. My feet felt so hot that I couldn't wear socks in my shoes. With every step and every waking moment, I experienced pain. This pain forced me to be so consumed with my struggle that I became self-centered. I knew it was affecting my Christian witness and my family to such a degree that I would fake happiness just to keep people from asking me questions. I was becoming a burden within myself because of my inability to focus on a task and see it through to completion. I hated this because I didn't want to be selfish, but I didn't know what to do. I didn't want to resort to drugs. In spite of the way I was feeling, I still believed in God.

I used to think if someone went through this kind of experience, it was his or her own fault. I would think, *Why can't you will it away through positive thinking or reading the Bible and praying? All you have to do is tell yourself to be happy, and you will make yourself happy.* I was so wrong. On top of everything else, I felt that guilt, complete humiliation, and unwanted selfishness were controlling my life. The burning sensation in my feet was alleviated with running cold water over them or walking in snow barefoot. Under normal circumstances, I couldn't stand walking in the snow barefoot, but when I was going through this pain, the snow would make my feet feel normal. I could stand in the snow, and it felt good.

I went to the doctor and submitted to a battery of tests. The results showed I had a disease college students get from drinking too much. The enzyme levels in my liver were elevated, and I had jaundice. I told him I didn't drink. I asked him what I could do to heal, and he told me, "You're forty, and stuff like this comes with middle age." Needless to say, this prognosis was not comforting or helpful. As time went on, the burning in my feet started moving up my legs; this made me more depressed. In the past, whenever I heard people talk about their depression and how sad and hopeless they felt, I would always wonder why they couldn't snap themselves out of it. Now that I was going through depression, I finally learned what these people were talking about. I know what it was like to feel completely hopeless with thousands of thoughts running in my head at one hundred miles an hour.

The thoughts wouldn't stop. They were unmanageable, yet they managed to consume me. Depression is a relentless barrage of negative voices that speak of doom without ceasing. When the sufferer doesn't sleep, it amplifies the negative feelings. Then things get worse because of the anxiety about being sleep deprived. When one can't sleep, everything bad becomes worse, causing a deeper panic and a paranoia to set in. I lost my appetite and was losing weight so fast that I was concerned that people would begin to notice and ask me if I were sick. This brought a sense that I was losing complete control and would eventually die.

While I was suffering in this depression, my twin brother, Ed, told me that I shouldn't be living life this way and should get my act together. I wanted to do everything he said, but I knew this depression was bigger than me because I was having such a hard time functioning. Even though my brother wanted to help me, his words made me feel worse. I prayed that the Lord would give him a glimpse of the pain I was feeling, barely believing my prayer would be heard because I felt so distant.

I didn't tell my brother that I had prayed that way. To my surprise, my twin brother started having some physical symptoms that caused him to worry about his own health. I could tell by our phone calls that he wasn't himself. He had a hard time expressing how he was feeling depressed. I think it's because when you're walking through it, you don't want anybody knowing you're battling with your own thoughts, and you feel out of control. After his short episode, the symptoms were alleviated, and his depression left. He called one day to apologize to me for the way he'd treated me through my own struggle. He said he wouldn't hassle me anymore about not having the joy of the Lord. I thanked him, and then I proceeded to tell him about my previous prayer. We still joke about how he doesn't want me to pray for him anymore.

All of these events were happening as I worked out the details of this new job offer in Florida. I made all the arrangements to move this time. I was trying to find the strength to function. We had gotten a lot further into the moving process, so far that I had already put down deposits for a moving truck and a condo in Naples. We had a moving sale at a friend's house to get rid of our winter clothes and things we wouldn't need in sunny Florida. We were deep enough into the process that my wife had quit her part-time job and had the house almost packed. We were about two weeks away from moving, and I had bought a ticket for my twin brother to come up and help me with the drive down.

Through the whole process, my wife told me to go get counseling. So I scheduled some time with my pastor, and it helped. I was still feeling all of the pressures of my sickness and was continuing my battle with depression during the moving preparations. The stress was so severe that the pain radiated up both legs. I was at my wit's end, and the fear of shutting down this move because of my inability to function in life was my greatest fear. I stuffed down those feelings because I was afraid of the repercussions of my wife's response. I felt terrible and horrified at the same time, but I knew the last thing I needed to do was to move.

I spent many nights outside, walking and praying, and asking God to deliver me; but it seemed like this depression would never leave. I finally told Pam we couldn't move. It was hard enough for me to do my present job, and the idea of starting a new job with new responsibilities, feeling the way I felt, made it unbearable. Once again, I stopped the moving process. When I made the decision, I felt completely relieved. I knew that we would have to suffer through all the repercussions and questions from people. I also knew it would be a painful course of events.

It would take awhile to restore my wife back into good standing with me and to heal from all the shortcomings and doubts that would arise as we worked through the recovery. I know this one thing: If God hadn't confirmed our marriage in such a dramatic way, and if we hadn't had him in our lives, our marriage probably would have ended. I am so thankful Jesus' sacrifice was sufficient to bring the resolution to the conflict we faced. We trusted if we held onto his hand through this storm and didn't let go, no matter how we felt, he would see us through to the victory and could heal us. It took time to recover and to restore trust in each other.

I came to the place in my life where I said, "It doesn't matter what happens to me. Whether I'm sick or I'm healthy, I am going to serve God; and I am going to serve him no matter what." Through thick or thin, living in depression and feeling pain or not, I told the Lord life goes on. I also told him that I couldn't keep living this way. After that, things started to change, and I started healing. The healing process took three to four years. I wanted instantaneous healing when it all started, and that's the way I prayed. By the end of the ordeal, my prayer was: "I don't care anymore what happens to me. God, you are still God, and I am the work of your hands. Take me and use me in whatever way you see fit." I think this prayer took away Satan's foothold in my mind, and the process of healing began because I surrendered myself fully to him even in my brokenness. Fear often assaults us because we are losing something or are afraid of losing something we want to cling to.

If we love our lives, we want to control the agenda. To our disappointment, when things don't go the way we planned or had hoped, it hurts; and we suffer pain and grief. The easiest way to say it is: the more surrendered we are to his lordship, the less life hurts, and the more fulfilled we will be living in his purposes. I wish it didn't take so long to learn certain lessons in life. I wish we could take a one-hour test, and it would be over. I think the Lord has to work through our emotional baggage to make things stick with us and build his character in us. That's why he sent the Holy Spirit to live in us for a lifetime; he knew it would take a lifetime for us to learn and mature.

Jesus' lessons take time, but if you have patience, you will benefit as you learn to surrender and serve him. Depression hurts, and I have felt that pain. Now that I know the pain, I can show mercy to those who struggle with depression; whereas before, I was critical and judgmental toward those who battled this disease. I know the Lord let me walk through this storm in my life to bring me to his way of loving people who are dealing with hardships. It saddened me that it took me so long to come to this understanding. Struggling with depression taught me God's love triumphs over everything, and it helped me to see that criticism only brings destruction.

BEING A DAD

ONE OF THE most important things in my life is being a father. I love being a father, and my main goal was to show my children the love of Jesus. I wanted them to know the same Jesus I had come to know, but I knew they wouldn't want to know my Jesus if they did not know my love first.

Kids have an uncanny ability to read between the lines, and they know when our hearts are truly in whatever we are trying to teach them. Their intuitive abilities aren't limited by intellect and pride, and they can see whether or not we are genuine or fake. How our kids respond to us is a barometer of how we are handling our relationships with them. If our relationship with our kids is strained, it is a telltale sign there might be an issue in us or our relationship that needs to be dealt with. If we are not listening and receiving messages from our own children in a spirit of humility, then they might use rebellious actions to get our attention.

We must remember as parents that the buck stops with us. We are the ones who need to change first in order to create a positive change in our kids. Jesus said in John 8:32, "Then you will know the truth, and the truth will set you free." The only way we can know the truth is to read it, and the only way we can be set free is to know and believe what it [God's Word] says is true. This is the biggest weakness in us: we don't know enough of the truth to be set free to live the life of liberty that is reflective of God's glory. Because of this, kids don't see enough freedom in their parents, so they create their own false freedoms through rebellion.

I am not a perfect father, but Jesus has all the answers in his Word. If we asked him for help, he would resolve every challenge we face. We must realize we know nothing apart from Jesus. I tell my kids that they were worth every penny I paid for them. They always get a chuckle from that, but I think they know what I mean. The Bible teaches in 2 Corinthians 3:6, "He has made us competent as ministers of a new covenant—not of the letter but of the Spirit; for the letter kills, but the Spirit gives life."

I know religion without genuine love means nothing. My kids knew I took my faith seriously because of the way I loved them. They also knew the way I loved them was because of my faith, so they learned the two went together: one without the other is dead. Our faith without love expressed toward those we love means nothing. (That's religion.) But our love should express how much our faith is of value to us. Our children see our faith by the way we love, and they know how much we love because of our faith. None of us can fake it; we have to be real. You can't have one without the other.

Religion by itself kills, and people can't follow it with true heartfelt devotion. The knowledge and acceptance of Jesus' love comes first, and that love changes people from the inside out and creates the motivation to action. We can only know this through brokenness of heart and acknowledgment of God's help in our lives. Only through true sincerity of heart can an invitation be offered for the Holy Spirit to take up residence. God will not jump over walls of pride to get into our hearts. He will knock them down so he can reign and rule within. He will not come in second. His is the gold medal. That's what makes him God and King.

JOSIAH DANIEL

I AM THE most blessed man in the whole world. At least, that's what I think. Jesus has blessed me with wonderful, faith-filled children. I have four marvelous children who are serving God. The Bible says in Proverbs 23:24, "The father of a righteous man has great joy; he who has a wise son delights in him." Wise children make a father happy. This success started when Jesus said to me the day my son was born, "You love your kids first. Then you tell them about me."

Josiah Daniel, our firstborn, has a very tender heart, but he protects it with a tough, sarcastic exterior. In getting to know him, it doesn't take long to figure out he is more bark than bite. He has a mind like a steel trap that remembers minute details. He is very observant. He knows his environments. While growing up, he made us aware of many life-threatening situations.

One incident happened before he was two and could speak fluently. Pam went outside to burn some trash. Then after the fire was lit, she started walking toward the house. Josiah stayed outside to play. We lived in the country at that time and had a huge yard. Just before Pam entered the house, she noticed a small whirlwind coming down the lane. After a few minutes, Josiah started beating on the screen door, saying, "Hot, hot, hot." Pam came to the door and saw the barn engulfed in flames. In shock, she called the fire department. This stirred up emotional memories from the Teen Challenge fire. No one was hurt, but the barn was a total loss.

When Josiah was three years old, he came down the stairs, walked by the television, pointed at it, and said, "Jesus is going to give us a VCR." To be nice, I agreed with him. He kept repeating this statement over a period of a couple weeks. I told Pam what he was saying about the VCR, and we both thought Jesus was telling us through our son he was going to provide the needed funds sometime in the future. Pam and I agreed that the next time we had an extra $300, we would buy a VCR for Josiah. I was naturally thinking it would be a long time before we would have enough money to make such a purchase. After another week or so, Josiah and I went to check the mail. When we got to the box, we opened it and found a letter from our close friends in Des Moines. They had felt the leading of the Holy Spirit to send us $300. I leaned over in excitement to tell Josiah that Jesus sent us the money for the new VCR. Josiah, in his childlike faith said, "Good," acting as if this were normal. When we got back to the house, we showed Pam the check, and we were all thanking God. Amazing!

One summer we attended the Iowa State Fair. When we arrived, the parking lot was full. I had to park a long way from the entrance. I dropped my family off relatively close to the entrance, and I continued to look for parking. As they were waiting for me to join them, the shuttle driver spied them and asked them if they would like a ride to the gate. Josiah, Rachel, and Becky were all standing next to Pam as she was holding onto the stroller that held Elizabeth. I was making my way toward them. As Pam was declining the shuttle service, she had taken her hands off the stroller, and it started rolling down a small incline toward one of the entry drives. Josiah, quick on his toes, grabbed the stroller before it got too far away. Thanks to Josiah, no one was hurt.

I've told him that he would make a great highway patrolman because he is so aware of everything going on around him. He is full of zeal for the things that interest him. He loves to read and learn. Josiah has a passion for technology. He knows his way around a computer like he knows the back of his hand, and he has been a huge blessing to his own family with all his technical skills.

When Josiah was a teenager, he was thinking about how things would be ten years into the future concerning technologies. He is a big-picture thinker and problem solver with strong organizational skills. I think the most successful attribute of Josiah's is his diligence. He never gives up once he starts a plan. He may get frustrated, but he keeps on going just like the Energizer Bunny.®

I believe with his big-time vision and diligence, he will be very successful in whatever he puts his hands to. He also likes to learn through experience. He doesn't want to take anyone's word for how something is; instead, he wants to live it for himself. He looks forward to living life and moving ahead. I think sometimes he feels life moves too slowly, and because of that, he has a hard time with patience. His zeal and his vision keep driving him to higher levels of success.

There was a time I felt like Josiah was getting to the place where he would make life-altering decisions that would influence the way he lived the rest of his life. I took the matter to the Lord with prayer and fasting. In prayer, I had a thought pass through my mind. I was seeing a time when Tom, a minister I knew, was coming to town to preach. Tom had a prophetic gift that he used liberally. I got up from my prayer time and checked his schedule on the Internet. To my surprise, I found out he was going to be in Fort Dodge the next day. So I asked Josiah if he was available to attend the meeting because I felt like the Holy Spirit had put it in my mind to take him to hear Tom speak. He said he was available and wanted to go.

The next day, Josiah came home from Des Moines, and we all went to hear Tom speak. While Tom preached, he would interrupt himself at times to give people prophetic words. In these prophetic words, the Holy Spirit would speak to a person's potential and how much God loves us. When Tom finished his preaching, he began to show a video of his ministry work in different countries all around the world. After the video was over, he called our family up front and pointed at Josiah. He said, "While you were watching the video, you were critiquing its quality and what changes could be done to make it better. You were thinking of all the technical things you could do to make it more professional and presentable." To Josiah's amazement, the missionary had pointed out exactly what he was thinking while he was watching the video.

After the service was over, Josiah told all of us he was impressed with the fact that God knew his thoughts, and it showed him how intimate and how powerful Jesus is. This experience emotionally time-stamped the greatness of God into Josiah's mind and has changed the way he looks at life and the kingdom of God. I am so thankful for Josiah and for the Holy Spirit's work in his heart and mind. I am thankful he is making decisions based on the advancement of the kingdom of God rather than the kingdom of self.

Later in Josiah's teen years, he found it hard to keep off the extra weight, and he continually added weight especially throughout his college years. His weight got to the place that Pam and I became concerned for his health. He had been on various diets in the past and was successful at losing weight only for a short time. Then he became frustrated and began to gain again.

One day, Josiah and I were able to strike up a conversation concerning the health issues that come with being overweight. I had a feeling that there was an underlying spiritual issue to the weight problem that we were not seeing, and I began asking God for wisdom. During our conversation, I asked Josiah if there was anyone he was holding resentment toward. He said no. I believed him. Then the seemingly random idea came to me that I should ask him if he had forgiven himself and God for making him overweight. When I looked at his face, his eyes lit up like it was Christmas. I said to him, "You go get ready for the day and ask God if you need to forgive yourself and God for your physical condition. Then we will meet upstairs at the kitchen table and pray together."

A few minutes later, I walked into the kitchen, and Josiah, tears streaming down his face, was already seated at the end of the table. He said, "Dad, that was it. I needed to forgive myself and stop blaming God." I was so happy to see the tears and the breakthrough. Before this time, we never thought this resentment was directed at himself and God. As soon as Josiah forgave, Jesus met him at his point of surrender. Josiah was thanking God out loud for the deliverance and the peace that filled his heart that day. He also mentioned how he felt so different after his surrender. He said it felt as if a tight band were taken off his head, and he also felt as if a literal weight had been lifted off his shoulders.

Josiah said that he felt his mind was finally at peace, and his thoughts stopped racing through his head. He was so accustomed to living that way, he thought it was the way God made him.

It is not until we are delivered of our demons that we know the true peace of God. Deliverance opens up a new intimacy and relationship with Jesus Christ. As I mentioned earlier, if we hold resentment toward anyone or anything, we will be held in a spiritual prison, locked up in chains, and the devil will be our tormentor until we forgive. Matthew 18:32-35 says:

> "Then the master called the servant in. 'You wicked servant,' he said, 'I canceled all that debt of yours because you begged me to. Shouldn't you have had mercy on your fellow servant just as I had on you?' In anger his master handed

him over to the jailers to be tortured, until he should pay back all he owed. This is how my heavenly Father will treat each of you unless you forgive your brother or sister from your heart."

The distinctive quality of Christianity is that we love our enemies. Matthew 5:43-48 says:

"You have heard that it was said, 'Love your neighbor and hate your enemy.' But I tell you, love your enemies and pray for those who persecute you, that you may be children of your Father in heaven. He causes his sun to rise on the evil and the good, and sends rain on the righteous and the unrighteous. If you love those who love you, what reward will you get? Are not even the tax collectors doing that? And if you greet only your own people, what are you doing more than others? Do not even pagans do that? Be perfect, therefore, as your heavenly Father is perfect."

Jesus commands us to forgive everyone including ourselves and God. If we have negative feelings toward anything or anyone, these negative emotions should be evaluated in the light of the truth. Then we can get out of prison and be delivered from our tormentors, and God will forgive us and give us the power to be in a place of joy. Remember if anyone has a reason to hold resentment, it is Jesus. He was perfect, and our sins sent him to the cross. Jesus did nothing wrong; however, he, in his perfect love, wanted to buy back his creation. Perfect love needed to provide a perfect sacrifice for a perfect plan of redemption. That perfect plan meant redemption for his creation including you and me. The gospel defines forgiveness, so we must learn to forgive daily those who offend us.

REBEKAH LYNNE

REBEKAH HAS NEVER faced a problem she couldn't tackle, starting with her heart condition before she was born and continuing with all the little scrapes, bumps, and bruises she got growing up. We gave her the nickname Becky Boo-Boo. While playing she would often be walking and talking, not paying attention to where she was going. Then she would run into things and get boo-boos—thus the name *Boo-boo*. When little Becky got tired, she might find me sitting in a chair. Grabbing her fuzzy wool sheep skin, she'd beeline to my lap and fall asleep. I have fond memories of those times. I can still see her cuddled there on my lap in her little onesie holding her wool fuzzy up under her nose as she gently dozed off.

When she was a little girl, we'd hear her talking to herself like she was carrying on a conversation with someone close to her. She had a little plastic phone and a briefcase with all her paperwork and office paraphernalia. She would set her briefcase down by me and then open it up to show me all the important work she had to do. Her little phone would "ring," and she'd answer it like a secretary who had high-level business to attend to. When the phone call ended, she would continue her business dialogue with me and anyone else who was interested. I was always impressed with her administrative skills and her ability to communicate details.

Rebekah has always blown me away with her innate understanding of fashion and hairstyles. Before she was three, she'd wake up in the morning, brush her long blond hair, and then show me, saying, "Pretty, pretty." I would say, "You are so beautiful," and then I would pick her up and give her a big hug; she was so cute. I was in awe at her ability to distinguish what blouse and skirt matched and which accessories were needed to complete the ensemble.

Speaking of ensembles, Becky is a connoisseur of purses. She required a purse for every outfit and occasion of her young life, and still does. I remember a time when we were preparing to go on vacation. I was packing the van, and Becky had brought me multiple suitcases—way more than an eight-year-old would require. I asked her why she needed so many suitcases, and she proceeded to tell me she needed all those suitcases because of all her outfits. I asked her what was in one of the suitcases, and she said, "Purses." I told her we couldn't take that many purses because we didn't have enough room in the van for all the bags. She would have none of it. She was convinced there was no way that she could wear what she had packed without a complete ensemble of accessories.

If my children had one rebellious moment, this would have been hers. There was no logical way, in her childish way of thinking, that she could wear any of the outfits without her matching purses. She made it known this was impossible, and she would feel incomplete if she wore anything without having a purse. After a few minutes of heated discussion, I won the battle and convinced her she would survive without all her purses on vacation. I told her she might lose one if she couldn't keep track of them. I think the idea of losing one scared her, so she was willing to compromise.

Rebekah is good at expressing her heart and feelings. She would be an excellent author. Writing comes so easily for her, and she can't understand why people have difficulty expressing themselves. This is a beautiful gift God has given her. If I ever wanted to know details about an event or something she attended, I knew I could trust her to retell the entire event with all of the particulars.

If I had to describe Rebekah with one character trait, it would be loyalty. Once Becky has decided what is right and what is wrong, she is loyal to that commitment. She is also loyal in her relationships with others, and her loyalty leads her to do the right thing even when it hurts. Her disappointment comes when people are not loyal with her. She has a hard time understanding why others don't feel the same way she does about being true and loyal.

Becky has grown into a beautiful, godly woman who wants to serve Jesus with all her heart. She loves to express this with design and in her writing because she is very creative and artistic.

While at college, Becky was confronted by the Holy Spirit challenging her to let go of past unforgiveness and hurts. We were doing one of our all-night drives from Iowa to Florida to take her back to school for her last semester. In one of our conversations on our long trip, I felt the Holy Spirit prompting me to tell her that she needed to make a list of everyone she held resentment toward.

When I said that (she told me later) her heart started racing, and people's names were coming to her mind. She knew it was the work of the Holy Spirit dealing with unresolved resentments in her heart. When she decided she was ready to be healed from the resentments of her past, Jesus met her at her point of surrender and began to pull out all the emotional pain. When Jesus revealed himself to her in such a dramatic way, she finally realized how intimate and personal a relationship with Jesus could be.

On that drive to Florida, after I had mentioned to Becky that she needed to make a list of the people she held resentment toward, we were coming up on some road construction near Chattanooga, Tennessee, necessitating all cars to merge. All the vehicles were in the left lane moving along at a pretty good clip. Eventually, all the cars were single file.

Up ahead, there was an onramp lane on the right coming into the main flow of traffic. I noticed a semi-truck loaded down with steel coming in on the ramp. He didn't notice the traffic was in a single lane, and I had no room to move to the left to make room for the merging semi-truck. It was about 1:00 in the morning. I was thinking he would slow down and wait for an opening so he could merge safely, but to our surprise, he made no attempt to slow down or check for traffic. Just as we were coming to the point of merger, he thrust himself into the main flow of traffic, and I had no alternative but to take the shoulder of the road to my left. Because of the construction, there was some loose gravel on the inside shoulder of I-75, so when I hit the gravel, the car began to fishtail back and forth. I did not want to take the median and get turned sideways causing the car to flip in the loose soil or perhaps get turned around and collide with the oncoming traffic.

While we were side-by-side, I thought I should speed up and get ahead of the truck. As I began to inch my way forward, the trucker started hitting his brakes, and because of this, we were able to get the car ahead of the truck, fishtailing the whole distance. As soon as we were ahead of the truck, I began to turn the car off the shoulder and back onto the pavement. The car began to fishtail, first to the left, then to the right, back and forth about five times. Then we began to spin around—probably five revolutions. While we were spinning and trying to keep the car on the pavement, we were taking out these tall, skinny pylons left and right. Becky's face was in her pillow, screaming, "Jesus, save us!"

During the commotion, I began to see the accident unfold. I felt as if I were seeing it before it happened. It was a surreal experience. I felt completely calm. I didn't say anything as the accident was unfolding, but I could see it playing out in my mind. I felt completely focused. I knew that the understanding and peace I was feeling was God, and he had his hand on us.

The car came to a screeching stop in the right lane near the right shoulder, on the opposite side of where we started, pointing toward oncoming traffic. The smell of burning rubber permeated the car. Becky and I both were overwhelmed with gratefulness. It was silent in the car as we sat there in shock, amazed that we were still alive. Then I looked over at Becky and took hold of her hand and asked her if she was okay. She nodded, too shocked to speak. I quickly got out of the car and did a walk-around to make sure nothing was bent severely and all the tires were still in place. Everything looked good, so I got back in the car, and we started down the road again. The traffic slowed down but didn't stop. I'm sure it was exciting to watch all the pylons flying through the air, but the show was over. We were thankful to be on the road again all in one piece. After a few minutes, I said, "Let's not tell Mom until we get to Florida, okay?" Becky agreed.

Later, it came to my mind that our discussion prior to the accident made the enemy mad, and he was out to destroy or diminish what was going on inside Becky's heart. He knew once she forgave everyone, he would no longer have a foothold in her life to stop God's blessing. Becky's story reminds me of the parable of the unmerciful servant in Matthew 18:21–35:

> Then Peter came to Jesus and asked, "Lord, how many times shall I forgive my brother when he sins against me? Up to seven times?" Jesus answered, "I tell you, not seven times, but seventy-seven times. Therefore, the kingdom of heaven is like a king who wanted to settle accounts with his servants. As he began the settlement, a man who owed him 10,000 talents was brought to him. Since he was not

able to pay, the master ordered that he and his wife and his children and all that he had be sold to repay the debt. The servant fell on his knees before him. 'Be patient with me,' he begged. 'I will pay back everything.' The servant's master took pity on him, canceled the debts and let him go. But when the servant went out, he found one of his fellow servants who owed him 100 denarii. He grabbed him and began to choke him. 'Pay back what you owe me!' he demanded. His fellow servant fell to his knees and begged him, 'Be patient with me, and I will pay you back.' But he refused. Instead, he went off and had the man thrown into prison until he could pay the debt. When the other servants saw what had happened, they were greatly distressed and went and told their master everything that had happened. Then the master called the servant in. 'You wicked servant,' he said. 'I canceled all that debt of yours because you begged me to. Shouldn't you have had mercy on your fellow servant just as I had mercy on you?' In anger his master turned him over to the jailers to be tortured, until he should pay back all he owed. This is how my heavenly Father will treat each of you unless you forgive your brother from your heart."

This passage says the jailer will torture us if we choose to hold onto our resentment. A lot of us hold onto our resentment because we think it is justified. We think because someone else did something to us that we did not deserve, we are just in our feelings of hurt. Most of us have lived with our pain so long it becomes a part of us, and then we wonder why God seems so distant. Sometimes we say to ourselves we already have forgiven those who have offended us. Or we can't allow ourselves to forgive them because that means they've won the battle.

In all reality, in our bitterness we are drinking poison hoping to kill someone else, and it is only killing us. We need to let go and let God heal us. We shouldn't lose sight of the high price that was paid through Jesus' death to forgive us all our sins when we didn't deserve it. Romans 5:8 says, "But God demonstrates his own love for us in this: while we were yet sinners Christ died for us." We must understand one of our sins was enough to send us to hell. If Christ, being perfect, died for us, how much more then should we, being imperfect, learn to forgive others.

We need to put everything into proper perspective. When we fixate on the hurt committed against us, we are blinded to our own sin. If we forgive, Jesus will pour out his grace to heal us and bring us to a new level of holiness. Then we can live above the storm and not in the storm. That's what holiness does; it separates us out of the storm so we can have the mind of Christ. If we whittled down the Gospel message to one word, it would be forgiveness. That's what Jesus did for us, so we must do this for others, and we must never lose this perspective.

Sometimes, we live in denial. We deny having unforgiveness so we won't have to confront our own pain. But, the Bible states that a man is known by his fruit. If there is unforgiveness, there will be less fruit. We would be much better off to be humble and brokenhearted before the Lord so we can be healed and delivered of our tormentors. Then God's abundant blessing would be liberally poured out into our lives. The goal is to stay out of prison. No one who is thinking rightly would send himself to prison to be tortured. As the Scripture says in Matthew 18:34, "The jailer will torture us." Not only will we be held captive, but Satan will have the right to torture us because we chose to break a spiritual law. It's bad enough being in prison, but in addition to being in prison, we will be tortured by the enemy. Think about it, a prisoner has no rights and no control over his life.

In the universe, God set spiritual laws so we may live orderly lives. He gives us the Bible so we can know what that order is. If we don't know the truth that's in the Bible, then there will be no order in our lives. Without law, there would be chaos. The truth in the Bible is designed to bring us to freedom from sin. The

Word of God will bring order to the person who is living by the truth.

In our lack of forgiveness, we are locked in chains—unable to live at our full, God-given potential. If we continue to believe the lie that we have no need to forgive others, then that lie has taken away our life. Let's take time to compare the two kingdoms. One is the kingdom of light, which is God's kingdom—a blessing. The other is the kingdom of darkness, which is the dominion of Satan. God's kingdom is based on perfect love. John 15:13 says, "Greater love has no one than this that he lay down his life for his friends." Jesus laid down his perfect life for us and now considers us his friends if we surrender to him. If God's love lives in us, then we will naturally bear fruit and affect those we come in contact with.

In Galatians 5:22–23, we find the fruit of the Spirit listed: "But the fruit of the Spirit is love, joy, peace, patience, kindness, goodness, faithfulness, gentleness and self-control. Against such things there is no law." The Bible teaches that if we are attached to the vine, we will bear fruit, and it will be good fruit. If believers are not attached to the vine, then there will be no fruit.

Jesus said in John 15:4–5:

> Remain in me, and I will remain in you. No branch can bear fruit by itself; it must remain in the vine. Neither can you bear fruit unless you remain in me. I am the vine; you are the branches. If a man remains in me and I in him, he will bear much fruit; apart from me you can do nothing.

Resentment will separate us from the vine if we do not forgive. Satan's kingdom is based on hatred. In Galatians 5:19–21 are listed the acts of the sinful nature. The acts of the sinful nature are obvious: "Sexual immorality, impurity and debauchery; idolatry and witchcraft; hatred, discord, jealousy, fits of rage, selfish ambition, dissensions, factions, envy, drunkenness, and orgies." Hatred made the list and is the basis from which many of these other acts of the sinful nature manifest themselves. If these acts are in our lives, then we know we have some changes that need to be made for us to be influential in the kingdom of God. It is in our best interest to surrender to the kingdom of God. God will give us the grace that we need to fulfill the purpose in our lives that would make our hearts sing.

Becky's relationship with the Lord grew tremendously in her college years. One night she called me and told me all the things the Holy Spirit was showing her and how she longed for God's presence in prayer. Through this, she began to realize how relationships with people don't compare with the presence of God and how important it is to have a personal relationship with the Creator of the universe through surrender. She had tasted the fruit of the presence of God and had been emotionally time-stamped in her heart. She was a different girl. I saw my little Becky growing into a mature, godly woman. The things of this world didn't satisfy her anymore; she had been brought to a new level of holiness and separation through the work of the Holy Spirit.

A higher call was on her life, and she could sense the change Jesus had started. I rejoiced to see my daughter not being satisfied by worldly and temporal things. She now saw the importance of sharing her faith. After graduation, Becky felt the Lord leading her to stay in Florida rather than take a job in her field of study. This step in faith led her to live in a place far from home, without a job in a struggling economy. God supernaturally provided for her for these months she lived on her own. When this change happened in her life, I received phone calls describing all the things God was doing in her and her friends. She would explain how God was using her to speak to other people and minister the truth of the Word of God. My daughter was completely different, and I was ecstatic about the positive change. Jesus proved himself miraculous because of her willingness to forgive.

RACHEL JOY

RACHEL JOY, OUR cute little screamer, seemed to have a lot of stomach pain when she was little. She spent a big part of her young life crying, though we did everything we could to calm her. It was understandably difficult at times. It didn't happen quickly, but she grew out of the crying and turned into a joyful little girl. At a young age, Rachel saw the importance of prayer. There was a gentleman in our church named Mike who had been diagnosed with leukemia; this was the same disease that took my father's life. When I found out Mike had the disease, I immediately said to Jesus, "Not again!" I immediately sent up a prayer for Mike. I shared the news with our family and asked them to join me in prayer for Mike's recovery. Rachel made it her own personal crusade to pray for Mike's healing. At every meal, Rachel would pray aloud for Jesus to heal Mike. This went on for a few months, and I was surprised by Rachel's consistency in her prayers for Mike. Rachel was focused on the things of God at a young age, which was unusual. After a few months, we heard the good news: Jesus miraculously healed Mike of leukemia. He is alive to this day and has experienced no reoccurrence. Praise God!

Rachel's interventions did not stop there. Ed, our neighbor, was a hardworking guy who had just moved to Iowa from Wisconsin because of a job transfer. Ed was a believer who struggled with smoking. Rachel was concerned about his cigarette smoking, so Rachel told Ed he should stop smoking because it was hurting him. Ed told her, "I want to quit, but I am having a hard time, and God really needs to help me." That statement put a seed in Rachel's heart, and she began to pray daily that Ed would have the strength to quit.

About a year later, we had Ed and his wife, Laura, over for a barbecue. Rachel walked up to Ed and asked him, "Do you still smoke cigarettes?"

Ed sweetly replied to her, "No, I don't, Rachel, thanks to you, your prayers and God's help." Rachel has never wavered in her faith; she has always seen the importance of having a relationship with Jesus. She has a strong sense of what's right and what's wrong. She truly brings joy to my heart.

Rachel has dark-brown eyes and dark-brown hair. She loves her daddy and always used to come to me for reassuring hugs. Whatever she was doing, she always had an eye on me. Sometimes I would glance at her in passing, and those little brown eyes were looking right at me. Much of her toddler life was spent using hand signals with me to get me to do things for her. I would remind her to use her words to communicate, but I liked her hand signals. We had a mutual understanding of what they meant and what she wanted. (I think most of the time she used them because she was a strong believer in pacifiers and didn't want to take her pacifier out of her mouth to talk.)

She was devastatingly cute with those dark, little eyes, and she used those eyes to peer into a person's soul. Little did we know she would grow up with a strong discerning ability. There would be times I would handle things incorrectly, and I could tell by her look I was wrong. She made it clear that I had crossed the line and that I needed to go back and fix my mistake. After I corrected the mistake, she would look at me with a smile of satisfaction.

When Rachel hugs me, she requires a two-armed hug, not a side hug or one-armed hug—those would not fly with her. When I do hug her, she will lift up her chin on my chest and peer at my face with those chocolate eyes. She likes looking at her daddy, and I like looking at her.

Rachel's laugh is one that is memorable. She definitely fulfilled her middle name Joy. Her laugh ignites laughter on whoever is around her. In high school, most of the notes in her yearbook mention how her laugh was the most memorable part of their friendship. At Rachel's wedding, the minister, Mark, commented that even when he is preaching at their church, he knows when Rachel is in attendance because he can hear her laugh over the thousand people sitting in the crowd.

Rachel was always rambunctious and adventurous. She would wander away from us when we were in public places, exploring new and unseen things. We had to keep an eye on her so she wouldn't get lost. While vacationing in Florida one winter, we went shopping with my brother's family. By accident, we had left Rachel in a store because she had wandered off, and we had not counted heads before leaving the store. When we noticed that she wasn't around, we hurried back to the store and found her sitting and crying on the counter, being comforted by the store clerk. She was a little traumatized and scared but really happy to see us, and we were so relieved. From that time on, she hung close by, never leaving the side of Pam or me. I never thought much about her reaction to the events of that day until she was older and I noticed that she seemed to be more fearful and afraid of change compared to my other kids.

Rachel and I had some conversations about the fear that she was feeling, and I tried to console her, not realizing that it could be a spiritual problem. A few years later, when she was preparing to go to college in the fall, she was telling me how afraid she was about going to school. I finally realized that she was abnormally fearful, so I told her that it was time to pray; and she agreed with me. So as we were sitting on the patio deck at her grandmother's house, I took my daughter's hands, and I looked her in the eyes and told her I was sorry for letting this go on so long. She peacefully forgave me, and we began to pray. I took authority over the spirit of fear and commanded it to leave her in Jesus' name. As soon as that was said, tears streamed down her face, and she looked peaceful. She was a new girl from that point on. She was completely healed, and later she told me she was looking forward to college and saw life as an adventure. Praise the Lord for his delivering power and for the keys he has given us to help set the captives free through his death and resurrection.

Rachel also spent a summer in North Myrtle Beach, South Carolina, on a mission trip working with Campus Crusade for Christ. We received a lot of phone calls from her during that summer that were very encouraging because of the things Jesus was doing in her heart. She said they would go to the beach, approach people, and share stories of the things God had done in their lives. She was surprised that most people would listen to her without shunning her. She called us one night and told us she had led two little girls to Jesus. She was so excited and encouraged by the way the Holy Spirit was speaking through her. She learned so much that summer and met a lot of new people. She told us this was a great learning experience and the trip had brought her out of her shell. Rachel would not have considered a trip away from home before being set free from fear. We were so blessed to watch her venture out in the loving hands of her heavenly father. The lessons learned while in South Carolina were a big step in her faith journey.

ELIZABETH BRIANNA

OUR YOUNGEST DAUGHTER is Elizabeth Brianna. Elizabeth came along six years after Rachel. We were all excited to know there was going to be a new baby, especially the little girls. When Elizabeth was born, she was such a pretty baby. She had bright blue eyes and was very content. She was easy to please and rarely cried.

As she grew older, she was always working on a project. Elizabeth would contentedly play by herself. When she was young, I worked evening hours, so I was able to spend the morning with her. She had to have a project to work on whether it was a game or a craft. One evening the Holy Spirit showed me a musical note inside her. As she has grown, this has proven to be true. She is a lover of all kinds of music and is always humming or singing a tune. She's always listening to music on her iPod and downloading the newest music for her listening pleasure.

Elizabeth was born with a merciful heart; she is loving and forgiving, and will give up what she desires to please others.

Whenever Elizabeth sees friends, they will always get a hug from her. Even now when some of her peers see her, they all scream her name in glee and seem ecstatic to see her. They know they will receive genuine love and concern from her—sealed with a hug. Elizabeth always does the things I ask of her without complaining or grumbling. I tell her that because she honors her father and mother in this way, God will truly bless her with a fruitful life. She is rarely grumpy, and she definitely defines what it is to love. Elizabeth desires to help children and be a blessing to everyone around her. When she was really young, Jesus showed her she would do missionary work and help children.

Every time I think of my daughter Elizabeth, I see her smiling, loving face and her arms stretched out toward me wanting a hug. If I were to define my daughter and her true heart in two words, they would be "love" and "mercy."

The Lord gave me three affectionate daughters who love to give hugs. He knew I cherished those hugs and needed them in my life. All my children are such a blessing to me and the rest of our family. I have encouraged my kids to experience life and become their own person. I am not a parent who wants my children to grow up and live around me all my life. I've wanted them to mature and become the most they can be and have a true experience with the Holy Spirit. As they have grown in their faith, Jesus has given them these true experiences. I have told them that the more they come into personal contact with Jesus, the less they will desire the things of this life. But, they must remember that they can't live on my faith for the rest of their lives. They must develop their own faith and live their own experience with Jesus. My responsibility is to pray that Jesus would reveal himself to them and nurture them in the Word of God, and to live my own life as open and real as possible. I live by faith so they can see by my actions what I believe, and the best way to show them Jesus is to live humbly by his Word.

We as parents must be able to let our children speak into our lives. They can see things we can't, and we must not let our pride stand in the way. We should learn to be approachable. If we respond in anger or are ill-tempered, they will avoid us like the plague. They will do things in a way we may not like to force us to listen to them. Pride is the destroyer of everything. It was the original sin and is the basis of every other sin. The humble road is always the best route; we must let our kids speak to us even if we don't want to hear what they have to say. Jesus will use them to speak truth to us and get our attention. The Bible teaches in 1 Corinthians 1:27, "But God chose the foolish things of the world to shame the wise; God chose the weak things of the world to shame the strong." We must be careful how we handle the things that he considers important. The most important thing to Jesus is people. The kingdom of God is about people. The only thing you can take to heaven with you is people; this alone shows us the value of people in God's heart.

THE HOLY SPIRIT

G OD WANTS TO be intimately involved in the lives of people through the Holy Spirit. Some people teach that the work of the Holy Spirit through spiritual gifts is not needed anymore. But, if the book of Acts is actually continuing in our lives today, this makes no logical sense. If the gifts of the Holy Spirit had not been working in our family and through the ministries we have been involved with, we would not be where we are today. To give you an example, when Rachel was a toddler and finances were tight, we received a prophetic word that God would not allow our appliances to wear out. This was an unspoken concern of Pam's because of our small income. Pam always wondered, *What if something happened?* As we looked at the numbers, we knew we would never be able to replace any of our appliances. To our whole family's amazement just a few years ago, we realized that we have given away or sold our appliances, all in working order. God's Word to us was true; we have never had an appliance wear out. Thank God for the gift of prophecy and all his other gifts.

Jesus sent his Spirit to be a comforter and teacher, and one of the ways he teaches us is through the conviction of our sin. The Holy Spirit convicts us so our eyes are opened to the truth about ourselves and just how sinful we are. Proverbs 16:2 says, "All a man's ways seem innocent to him, but motives are weighed by the Lord." It is the Holy Spirit's job to equip us for the work of God here on this earth; and without this conviction, we'd be sinful and ill-equipped. The Holy Spirit nudges and speaks to us individually. He deals with each one of us differently. Just as there are many gifts of the spirit, each gift is used at the perfect time for that individual. He is so intimate; he knows exactly how to deal with us right where we are. All the Holy Spirit needs is a believer who is open to the gifts of the spirit and willing to speak out in faith.

We are God's tools. In Ephesians 2:10 it says, "For we are God's workmanship, created in Christ Jesus to do good works, which God prepared in advance for us to do." I remember a time when I wanted the Lord to speak through me, but I was afraid. Even though I was eager to be used, I still had a hard time believing that God wanted to use me. I felt like the Holy Spirit was telling me to give someone encouragement about something, and I didn't say anything to him because of the fear of rejection. I have since learned that if people reject what the Lord is saying through me, they are rejecting him. Luke 10:16 says, "Whoever listens to you listens to me; whoever rejects you rejects me; but whoever rejects me rejects him who sent me."

Once when I was filling in for a pastor friend of mine, the elders wanted to pray for me just as the service was starting. I agreed and followed them into the pastor's office. They began to pray for me that God would minister by his Holy Spirit the word of truth. After they were finished praying, they told me the pastor normally prays for people before he begins preaching.

They requested I pray for people the same way. I struggled with that request because I wasn't accustomed to praying for people publically, and I was new at this preaching thing. I reluctantly agreed to pray. The worship service had started, and during the songs I worried about how I would pray for everyone. After the worship time, one of the elders announced that everyone who needed prayer should come forward so we could pray for them. About ten people came forward. On my way to the altar, I was gently reminded that I was the one who had asked God to use me. I wanted the Holy Spirit to speak through me, so right there I decided to be open to whatever I felt the Lord leading me to do—no matter how I felt. It wasn't about me, and I needed to remember that if I wanted to be God's messenger, I had to let him speak through me.

In faith, I walked up to the first couple and began to pray. Nothing specific was coming to mind, so I started to move to the next person. Then the thought came to me that I should go back and pray for healing in the wife of the couple I'd just prayed for. I slowly stepped back and prayed Jesus would heal her, and I rebuked the sickness in her body. After I had finished praying for them, the husband wanted to say a few words. I handed him the microphone, and he encouraged everyone in the congregation who needed or wanted prayer for healing to come forward for ministry. With tears welling up in his eyes, he began to tell them Jesus was ministering through the gifts of the Holy Spirit and had given them hope and reassurance of his goodness. Then he looked at me, his eyes wet with thankfulness, and handed the microphone back to me. I proceeded to pray for all those who had come up for ministry.

A couple of days later, I found out through someone in the church that the elder's wife I had prayed for had been diagnosed with breast cancer and that they were very encouraged by the word of the Lord that had been spoken to them. That word gave them the faith to believe she was healed of the disease. To this day, this woman is alive and cancer-free. Praise Jesus for his healing power! The work of the Holy Spirit continues in the lives of those who pursue its operation. The only things that stand in our way are pride and the walls we have built with bricks of intellect.

When a person functions in the gifts of the Holy Spirit, most times he won't have understanding of the picture he sees in his mind or of the word given to speak in faith. I think God does it this way so we can't process it with our own thinking. If we could process it, then we might take ownership of the gift, thinking it originated with us. This would be dangerous thinking because nothing God does through us originates with us. We are mere vessels. Jesus, the creator of the universe, doesn't need us; but he wants to use us because he loves us. Jesus wants us to be empty vessels for his purposes. When we know the gifts originate with him, we can't have pride. He doesn't want us to process what's happening in the person we are ministering to; he wants faith from us. Faith is the only thing that pleases God. It says in Hebrews 11:27, "And without faith it is impossible to please God, because anyone who comes to him must believe that he exists and that he rewards those who earnestly seek him." I know using the gifts of the Holy Spirit in our day-to-day lives is how Jesus helped Pam and me raise our children and deal with our family issues. Without the Holy Spirit's daily interaction, our family would not be what it is today. My kids tell me frequently that things I have spoken to them through the Holy Spirit, sometimes unknowingly, brought answers to questions and peace to many situations concerning them.

When the children were small (elementary age) our nightly routine was to read a story, talk and pray. During my prayer, I would sometimes speak in my prayer language over them. They asked me questions about the gift and wanted to try it for themselves. Pam and I explained how I received the gift of tongues when I was in college. I told them how I had made the decision to be open to receiving the gift of tongues. I explained my act of speaking aloud syllables by faith, believing God would give me more syllables through my step in faith.

I asked them if they wanted to step out and receive this gift for themselves. They all said yes, so I said we would agree in prayer together. I said, "I want you to take a step in faith and begin to speak out the syllables, trusting God to allow the gift to flow through you." I could see the anticipation and excitement on their faces as I held all their hands and began to pray with them that Jesus would speak through them. I told them Jesus needed to use their lips, their tongues, and their voices. I said, "You can't wait for him to take you over like a robot. He wants to use you as you submit your voice and tongue to him. I asked them if they understood what I was saying, and they all nodded. Pam and I quietly began to speak in our prayer languages to encourage them to make the step in faith.

They timidly began to pray barely audibly. I encouraged them to speak louder and to ignore the thoughts in their heads telling them this was stupid. As I did so, they began to get louder. As they were doing this, they began to say syllables that weren't in their heads. They realized that they were saying things that didn't originate with them or make sense to them. They were beginning to get excited and talk louder as the gift began to bubble out of them. We rejoiced in the smiles developing on their faces as they heard God speaking through them. They were so happy and excited God had given them the ability to use this new gift. It was an exciting night for all of us. The kids were young enough in their faith that they accepted things easily. They trusted their dad enough to believe what I was telling them was the truth, and because of that, they were able to receive their prayer language without a lot of mental processing.

Jesus said in Matthew 18:3, "I tell you the truth, unless you change and become like little children, you will never enter the kingdom of heaven." He also reminded his disciples of this many times. When we are young, we believe what we are told and accept it without analyzing everything. This is why we must surrender our thinking to a God who sees the whole picture. If we are dead to ourselves, then God can use us in ways we could not have dreamed of on our own. Jesus wants his dreams to come true for us, but we first have to accept, like a child, that he is able. My children trusted me as their father when I was teaching them about speaking in tongues. They knew I, like our heavenly father, would not steer them into harm's way. Jeremiah 29:11 says, "'For I know the plans I have for you,' declares the Lord, 'plans to prosper you and not to harm you, plans to give you hope and a future.'"

As we get older, we tend to accumulate emotional baggage and tradition that stand in the way of child-like faith. If we do not allow the work of the Holy Spirit to heal our lives, we will become stagnant and of no use to him and his kingdom. 2 Corinthians 4:7 says, "But we have this treasure in jars of clay to show that this all-surpassing power is from God and not from us." It is the will of God for us to receive from the ministry of the Holy Spirit, so we will be healed of our past hurts and disappointments. He desires for us to be empty vessels ready to be filled with whatever treasure he chooses. We need to get over ourselves. And unless we choose to do so, we will continue to be derailed trains—no good to anyone.

My admonition to you is always to be in a state of brokenness before God. When we are broken, understanding just how helpless we are without him, we no longer *want* to rely on our own thinking. We begin to swallow the fact that every single breath is a gift from God, and it is because of him we are allowed to do anything at all.

2 Corinthians 1:8-9 says:

> We do not want you to be uninformed, brothers, about the hardships we suffered... We were under great pressure, far beyond our ability to endure, so that we despaired even of life. Indeed, in our hearts we felt the sentence of death. But

this happened that we might not rely on ourselves but on God, who raises the dead.

This life is not easy, and being a Christian means dying to self, every day. In Luke 9:23 it says, "Whoever wants to be my disciple must deny themselves and take up their cross daily and follow me." The things of this world were not ever intended for us to endure alone. That is why God sent the Holy Spirit. But these hard times are allowed to present themselves so we never forget that we must rely on Jesus Christ because he has power even to raise the dead!

My encouragement to all of us is to study the Word of God. Know what God says and thinks about you. This is your ammunition for this life. Seek to understand that spiritual gifts are for you today. God gave them as weapons. Without them, the war zone is a lot bloodier. The Bible teaches in 1 John 4:4, "You, dear children, are from God and have overcome them, because the one who is in you is greater than the one who is in the world." After spending time in India, my eyes were opened to just how hidden spiritual warfare is in the Western hemisphere. The devil's work is incognito because we try to assent intellectually to God and fix things ourselves.

2 Corinthians 10:4 says, "The weapons we fight with are not the weapons of the world. On the contrary, they have divine power to demolish strongholds." This teaches that we are in a spiritual war, and the weapons of our warfare are not in the realm of what we can see with our eyes. Whether we see it or not, every day is a battle. Every negative word, disease, lie, and ache is not from God. He is good. He would never hurt us, but we live in a sinful world. And through our sin, we open up doors for the enemy to step in and create strongholds. These strongholds are so clever that we ourselves can be deceived by the root of the sins that plague us. Most strongholds reside in our minds and are rooted in pride or seated on a lie or some thought or belief

that does not agree with the Word of God. Satan came that he might steal, kill, and destroy (John 10:10). This is the character of our enemy. He will do whatever he can to steal from you, lie to you, and destroy your life. He would kill you immediately, if God would allow it. We need to open up our eyes and start standing up and fighting for what is rightfully ours!

I was not raised in the church, so I couldn't rely on what people had taught me concerning my faith. Most of my early influences were through reading the Bible. The acceptance of Biblical truth came more easily to me because I wasn't filled with all the preconceived ideas presented in church doctrine. I knew nothing about the Bible or Christianity. All I knew was I became a new person, and something changed in me. This experience created in me a desire to know more of the truth. I was fascinated with the Bible and this new dimension of living. I had to know more about this Jesus and what he wanted me to do with my life. I had no reservations about submitting to the will of God because what it had to offer was so much better than the life I left behind.

I knew I had the ability to screw up my life, and I was tired of that. I needed more than what I was presently experiencing. My logical mind also understood that if God is God, then he knows everything, and he can see from the beginning to the end. He knew exactly how I fit into his plan. It was easy for me to submit to his purpose because I felt like I was on a slow-moving train going nowhere. When I realized I was in the arms of Jesus, my perspective changed; and I knew that God would direct me down the right path.

I must admit there have been times since becoming a Christian when I have wondered where God was and what he was doing in my life. As I have grown older (and hopefully wiser) I have sensed a greater need and desire to take on a bigger role in the fulfillment of the great commission. When Jesus comes back for his bride, I want to be found the faithful and wise servant who made himself ready for his appearance. I know everything I do in this life will have an eternal value placed on it. It is my desire to finish the race I have been called to run and win the prize.

My prayer for you is that you will be encouraged to live the life of faith and walk in the fulfillment of his purpose for your life—a life filled to the fullest, overflowing, and abundant. I pray that my life story and the beautiful acts of God I have experienced will help you come to a new level of faith in God's ability to work in you and for you. He wants to prove himself to you. He wants to amaze you with his wonders and astound you with his love. But, you have to open yourself up enough and give him an opportunity. I know one thing for sure: there is always more of God to be revealed in our lives no matter where we are on the ruler of faith. We will never completely arrive as long as we are in this life on earth. There is a constant revelation waiting to be shown to us if we desire to receive it. There are bigger and better dreams waiting to come true. My desire is for more of God in me. This is what's amazing about having a relationship with the Creator of the universe. Life is an adventure, and there is something new around every corner; all we have to do is surrender. Let's take a dive of faith together and begin to live in a place where dreams come true.